IN THE SAME SERIES

T0266114

DAIRY PROCESSING

Food Cycle Technology Source Books

DAIRY PROCESSING

Practical Action Publishing Ltd
27a Albert Street, Rugby, CV21 2SG, Warwickshire, UK
www.practicalactionpublishing.org

First published 1996\Digitised 2008

ISBN 10: 1 85339 335 5
ISBN 13: 9781853393358
ISBN Library Ebook: 9781780444000
Book DOI: http://dx.doi.org/10.3362/9781780444000

Since 1974, Practical Action Publishing has published and disseminated books and
information in support of international development work throughout the world.
Practical Action Publishing is a trading name of Practical Action Publishing Ltd
(Company Reg. No. 1159018), the wholly owned publishing company of Practical
Action. Practical Action Publishing trades only in support of its parent charity
objectives and any profits are covenanted back to Practical Action (Charity Reg.
No. 247257, Group VAT Registration No. 880 9924 76).

Illustrations by Matthew Whitton, UK
Typeset by Dorwyn Ltd, Rowlands Castle, Hants, UK

Contents

Preface

This source book is one of a continuing UNIFEM series which aims to increase aware-
ness of the range of technological options and sources of expertise, as well as indicating
the complex nature of designing and successfully implementing technology development and dissemination programmes.

UNIFEM was established in 1976, and is an autonomous body associated since 1984
with the United Nations Development Programme. UNIFEM seeks to free women from
underproductive tasks and augment the productivity of their work as a means of accel-
erating the development process. It does this through funding specific women's projects
which yield direct benefits and through actions directed to ensure that all development
policies, plans, programmes and projects take account of the needs of women producers.

In recognition of women's special roles in the production, processing, storage, preparation and marketing of food, UNIFEM initiated a Food Cycle Technology project in
1985 with the aim of promoting the widespread diffusion of tested technologies to
increase the productivity of women's labour in this sector. While global in perspective,
the initial phase of the project was implemented in Africa in view of the concern over
food security in many countries of the region.

A careful evaluation of the African experience in the final phase of this five-year
programme showed that there was a need for catalytic interventions which would lead
to an enabling environment in which women would have easier access to technologies.
This would be an environment where women producers could obtain information on the
available technologies, have the capacity to analyse such information, make technological choices on their own, and acquire credit and training to enable the purchase and
operation of the technology of their choice. This UNIFEM source book series aims to
facilitate the building of such an environment.

Acknowledgements

This series of food cycle technology source books had been prepared at Intermediate Technology (IT) in the United Kingdom within the context of UNIFEM's Women and Food Cycle Technologies specialization. During the preparation process the project staff have contacted numerous project directors, rural development agencies, technology centres, women's organizations, equipment manufacturers and researchers in all parts of the world.

The authors wish to thank the many agencies and individuals who have contributed to the preparation of this source book. Special thanks are owed to Clare Sheffield for preparation of the manuscript, Maria Soledad Lago of Grupo De Investigaciones Agrarias (GIA), Santiago, Chile, and Ilse Marks of UNIFEM for their contributions to the case study material, and Matthew Whitton for the illustrations. In addition to those listed in the Institutions section, the authors would also like to thank Josef Dubach, Bert Dingemanns of the Small-Scale Dairy Technology Group in the Netherlands, Marion Hamilton, Cathy Watson, Emma Crewe and Peter Fellows of IT for their invaluable contributions.

The preparation of the first five source books was funded by UNIFEM with cost-sharing contributions from the Government of Italy and the Government of the Netherlands. The Government of Italy provided the funds for the continuation of the series, as well as the translation into French and Portuguese and the printing of the first editions.

Sylvia Aguhob
Food Technology Centre,
College of Agriculture, Xavier University,
Cagayan de Oro City
The Philippines

Barrie Axtell
IT Consultants, Rugby, UK

Introduction

THE TROPICAL CLIMATE of many countries makes the manufacture and ripening of cheese very difficult and the storage of butter equally so. Outside Europe, there is little evidence of cheese and other dairy products in the traditional diet. In some parts of Africa, cattle were not used for milking until the Europeans came. In Latin America dairying appears to have been unknown until the coming, 500 years ago, of Europeans who brought with them both the animals and the technology. Even then, the animals were mostly used for meat.

Today, dairy processing in most developing countries has progressed very little and remains a domestic kitchen activity. Traditional products that have been developed take into account the local situation, available technologies and cultural habits. Except for a few areas where collective milk processing has been organized, the small quantity of milk produced by individual farmers, mostly scattered over a wide area, ensures that traditional dairy processing remains at the household level.

Dairy processing is traditionally the work of women as, before mechanization, it began in one of women's main domains, the kitchen. Home dairying is still a very important household activity in many countries. It contributes substantially to household income and in addition provides good nutrition and increased food security for the family.

Women continue to play a crucial and important role in the small-scale dairy sector and its development. Since milking and milk processing have always been the work of women, it is no wonder that many of the experienced workers in cheese factories, for example in Ecuador, are women (Dubach, 1992). In France, as in many parts of the world, a number of famous cheeses were developed by women, including Marie Hardel, the originator of the now world-famous Camembert cheese in 1792 (Carr, 1991). Among the pastoralists of Africa and small-scale family farms of India, it is the women who do the milking and processing into products such as cheese, butter or ghee. As the quantity of milk is small, this is done in the kitchen or outside the tent using traditional utensils such as calabashes or goatskins for churning butter, and mat filters to drain the whey when making cheese. Sometimes, milk is collected over a period of two to three days to increase the volume before any processing is done. Hygienic conditions are difficult to maintain where there is a scarcity of water and other basic resources. Ideas about sanitation may also depend on local beliefs, for example in India where the cow is considered to be holy and clean. In many rural areas women are, through poverty and lack of time, still denied access to formal education on basic hygiene and nutrition.

In most cases, women's tasks also include the marketing of dairy products and any surplus milk the family may have. They play a significant role in supplying villages with milk and milk products produced by their herds and processed in their own kitchens. In many societies, women also take care of the feeding, watering and general management of the herd, a task shared with children when they are not in school.

With the trend towards larger-scale milk collection systems, and bigger processing units, many women are likely to lose family income from traditional milk processing as they are placed under increasing competition by larger processors. It is therefore very important that traditional women processors have access to information that allows them to improve their efficiency and the quality of their products.

1
Milk processing

THE PERISHABLE NATURE of milk means that some form of processing is necessary to extend its shelf-life, transform it into different products to expand its market and to generate income by adding value. Ordinary heat treatment or pasteurization, while destroying harmful bacteria, does not make milk absolutely free from spoilage organisms. In a tropical climate, milk becomes unfit for human consumption within a day or two.

Processing milk into dairy products makes it more stable for storage over extended periods of time. In the tropics where ambient temperatures are high and refrigeration is not readily available, milk may be concentrated by boiling or made into butter, ghee or other products which keep better at room temperatures. When there is an abundant local supply, storage and marketing may have a low priority, leading to wastage. Processing helps eliminate wastage and also adds value.

In many tropical areas, there is a cultural reluctance to use fresh milk, which probably derives from safety considerations. In Africa and Asia, lactose intolerance (an inability to digest milk sugar) is common.

The consumption of fermented cheeses and yoghurts, in which the lactose has been converted into lactic acid, has helped reduce the problem. The limited market for liquid milk is a problem which can thus be remedied by creating a demand for processed milk products. Through community milk centres, such processing can create jobs, while at the home level it provides added income for the family.

General methods of milk processing

While there are numerous ways of processing milk that vary in detail, they can be classified into three broad areas. These areas may overlap and a combination of the two main methods may be used to make a better preserved product.

The first general method involves *increasing the acidity* (or lowering the milk pH). This slows down, or may prevent, the growth of spoilage micro-organisms and the action of enzymes (natural substances that cause changes in flavour, etc.). Increasing the milk's acidity can be achieved by:

o lactic acid fermentation: beneficial micro-organisms ferment the milk sugar, turning lactose to lactic acid.
o the addition of organic acids: for example, vinegar or lime juice.

The second method involves *lowering the moisture content* to a level which is sufficiently low to control the growth of micro-organisms and the action of enzymes, so making the product more stable. Moisture content can be lowered by:

o evaporation of water using heat;
o curdling the milk and removing the whey, or watery part, as in the case of cheese;
o mechanical separation of the fat by churning, in the making of butter;
o adding salt and sugar to bind part of the water as in the salting of cheese or making milk sweets;
o sun or air drying of products such as cheeses or milk casein, the milk protein;

o mechanical drying, for example roller and spray-dried milk powders.

The third method simply involves *heating* to produce either pasteurized or sterilized milk.

Milk composition

Milk contains the essential nutrients in the right proportions necessary to support a young mammal in the first stages of its life. It is a good source of carbohydrate, fat and protein as well as many vitamins and minerals.

The composition of milk varies from one species to another. In most countries, the principal source of milk is the cow but other animals such as goats, sheep, buffaloes, camels and yaks are also raised for milk production, particularly in the tropics. Table 1 shows the milk composition in various mammals.

Milk composition within a particular species also varies according to such factors as breed, the type of feed and nutritional status of the animal, stage of lactation and milking and the effects of changes in season.

Milk fat

The value of milk is influenced by its fat content and most collective milk purchasing schemes pay farmers based on fat levels. Milk with high fat content is creamy and smooth and yields more butter and cheese. It also contains more fat-soluble vitamins such as A, D, and E and provides a good source of energy.

Milk protein

From a nutritional point of view, milk is a very valuable source of high quality protein. This protein is mainly casein together with minor amounts of other proteins called albumin and globulin which are essential for disease resistance in the young. These last two are lost in the whey during cheese processing, while the casein is coagulated and therefore stays in the milk solids.

Lactose

Lactose is the main sugar present in milk. It gives milk its sweet taste. Some individuals are unable to digest lactose, most commonly in countries without a dairy tradition.

Table 1. Average percentage composition of milks of various mammals

Species	Water	Fat	Protein	Lactose	Minerals
Human	87.43	3.75	1.63	6.98	0.21
Cow	87.20	3.7	3.5	4.9	0.7
Goat	87.00	4.25	3.52	4.27	0.86
Sheep	80.71	7.9	5.23	4.81	0.9
Indian buffalo	82.76	7.38	3.6	5.48	0.78
Camel	87.61	5.38	2.98	3.26	0.7
Horse	89.04	1.59	2.69	6.14	0.51
Llama	86.55	3.15	3.9	5.6	0.8
Yak	82.5	8.0	–	–	–

Source: Webb, Johnson & Alford, 1974: FAO, 1990

Lactose is also important in the production of yoghurt and cheese since, as it is fermented to lactic acid, the milk becomes sour. The increased acidity then causes coagulation of the casein.

Minerals

Milk contains important minerals such as calcium and phosphorus which are necessary for the growth and repair of teeth and bones. A number of other minerals are also present in trace amounts.

Water

Milk has an average water content of 87 per cent. This is the medium in which water-soluble components of milk are dissolved, including the water-soluble vitamins such as B complex and C. Since the bulk of milk is water, its removal reduces the volume significantly which can help overcome transport and bulk storage problems. The effect on the nutritional quality depends on the method used.

Microbiology of milk

As milk is a highly perishable commodity whose composition is ideal for the growth of spoilage micro-organisms, a basic understanding of milk microbiology is important when considering any improvement to processing.

The high moisture content, abundant supply of nutrients combined with the almost neutral acidity (pH 6.7) and temperature of raw milk make it a very good medium for the growth of micro-organisms including those that cause food poisoning and for enzymatic changes such as those that cause rancidity in milk fat.

The types of micro-organisms that occur in milk can be divided into three broad groups:

o those that cause milk spoilage;
o those that cause infection in humans, called pathogens;
o beneficial micro-organisms such as those which bring about the natural fermentation of lactose to lactic acid. These are used by milk processors to prepare products such as cheeses and yoghurts.

Sources of contamination

Micro-organisms are found everywhere on animals and people, in the air, soil, water and milk. Good quality, safe milk is the result of good sanitary practices being observed throughout the entire process from milking through processing to packaging. The number of bacteria present in the end-product reflects the sanitary conditions under which the milk has been processed. It also indicates the storage life of milk or its products. The main sources of contamination by micro-organisms in raw milk are the surfaces, such as udder and utensils, which it contacts. The hands also convey bacteria to the milk during handling. This means that it is very important to clean hands and surfaces carefully with clean water. Improving sanitary practices during traditional milk handling and processing may meet resistance because of cultural beliefs or simply lack of time. Ideally, training of a practical nature is needed to demonstrate the effect of improved sanitation on product quality.

The udder
Milk inside a healthy udder contains relatively few micro-organisms. The external surface of the udder, however, harbours a large number of micro-organisms. Dirt such as dried mud, dung on fodder and hair can pass millions of bacteria into the milk. Good milking practice and cleanliness of the udder is vital. In addition, if

the animal is suffering from infections such as mastitis, the milk will contain harmful pathogenic micro-organisms.

The whole area of herd management and milking techniques is beyond the scope of this source book. It is strongly recommended that those advising projects involved in milk processing should seek advice from specialists in herd management, as good quality products can never be made from poor quality raw milk.

Equipment and utensils

All dairy utensils such as buckets, milking cans and filters accumulate spoilage organisms if they are not thoroughly cleaned and disinfected after each use. Equipment that is made of wood or to a design which is not smooth, with, for example, joints and corners, is very difficult to clean and provides possible places for micro-organisms to survive. Cloth filters must be properly washed and dried, in the sun if possible, after each use.

The milkers

As the milkers move from one animal to the next, they can transfer pathogenic micro-organisms to all the animals in the herd so that all the milk may become contaminated. A person who is suffering from an infection could thus infect the milk, making it unsafe for consumption.

The milkers play a vital role in controlling the level of sanitation. They can directly check the cleanliness of the premises and utensils and observe the health and cleanliness of the animals as well as their own personal hygiene.

The environment

The environment in and around the milking premises affects the level of contamination in milk. If milking is done inside the stable, as is usually the case

with small farmers, there is a high risk of contamination through the air and insects, particularly flies. It is therefore better to milk in a special parlour but if this is impossible, milking in the pasture is preferable to the stable. Utensils containing milk should be kept covered whenever possible.

Water supply

Using polluted water to wash udders, utensils, etc. will cause contamination. A clean water supply is essential to minimize contamination. Some water-borne bacteria are dangerous. Coliforms, which cause stomach disorders in humans, also cause quality defects in dairy products such as cheese. Cholera, another water-borne disease, can cause death. If a supply of clean drinking water is not locally available, water quality can be substantially improved by adding a small quantity of household bleach to water used in the dairy (approximately five drops per gallon or one drop per litre). Alternatively, the water can be boiled, although this uses a considerable amount of fuel.

Once micro-organisms have found their way into milk, they develop easily and multiply rapidly. Micro-organisms grow best at room temperatures, so keeping milk cool will slow down their growth. Heating the milk, a process known as pasteurization, destroys a large number of the micro-organisms. This is described in Chapter 3. Also, making the milk more acid, either by natural fermentation or the addition of acid, suppresses the growth of harmful organisms.

Classification of milk products

Across the world, a wide variety of food products are derived from milk. While

Table 2. Classification of cheese according to moisture content

Type	Moisture (%)	Fat (%)	Texture	Shelf-life
Soft cheese	45–75	up to 40	Soft and spreadable	A few days
Semi-hard cheese	35–45	up to 35	Firm to crumbly, can be sliced	A few months
Hard cheese	30–40	up to 30	Very firm, dense, sometimes grainy	One year or more

they vary from one place to another as they are adapted to suit local conditions and available resources, they can be classified broadly as cheeses, butters, creams, fermented milks and miscellaneous products.

Cheeses

These can either be fresh or ripened by an ageing process. They are made by coagulating the milk and draining off the liquid whey. Cheese is a concentrated food containing practically all the valuable nutrients originally found in the liquid milk. The coagulation can be carried out in several ways. The most common practice involves adding rennet, a natural enzyme found in the fourth stomach of a ruminant. In some situations the milk is coagulated by adding an acid such as vinegar or vegetable enzyme extracts. The final characteristic of the cheese depends in part upon the particular type of coagulant used.

There are more than a thousand varieties of cheese all over the world and there is no absolute method of classification. Classifications are based on several properties and characteristics, such as fat content, source of milk, method of coagulation, and whether ripened or unripened. A simple and commonly used method is according to the moisture content as summarized in Table 2.

Butters

These are made from the fat component of whole milk which is dispersed as very small invisible globules. In buttermaking, the fat globules are made to join together through mechanical agitation. The fat forms a semi-solid mass with 80–85 per cent fat and up to 16 per cent water. Various types of butter and butter-like products are made from either fresh or soured milk. In some cases salt is added, in others the butter is allowed to ripen. In some countries the moisture content is reduced by heating to give a more stable product, known as clarified butter or ghee. The characteristics of common butters are shown in Table 3.

Table 3. Types of butter

Type of butter	Description
Fresh butter	Mild, creamy flavour, unsalted, unripened.
Fresh salted butter	Salted (1–8%), unripened.
Cultured butter	Made from soured whole milk or cream. Slightly acid taste. May be salted or unsalted.
Whey butter	A butter produced from the whey after making cheese. Slightly acid, salted or unsalted.
Ghee	A pure fat made by heating butter to remove the moisture.

Table 4. Types of fermented milks

Type	Starter	Description
Yoghurt, set yoghurt, stirred yoghurt	*Lactobacillus bulgaricus, Streptococcus thermophilus*	Made from whole milk, skimmed milk or dry milk powder. Gel-like when set; creamy, highly viscous when stirred.
Cultured buttermilk	*S. cremoris, S. lactis, S. diacetilactis, Leuconostoc citrovorum.*	Made from left-over skimmed milk, from butter-making. Can have a strong acidic flavour. Liquid.
Acidophilus milk	*Lactobacillus acidophilus*	Liquid, acidic flavour.
Kefir	*S. lactis*, Torula yeast, *Betabacterium caucasicum*	Slightly fizzy and slightly alcoholic soured milk.

Fermented milks

These are acidified or soured milks produced by the natural fermentation of lactose to lactic acid or by the addition of a starter culture (a previously prepared or commercially produced bacterial culture of selected micro-organisms). The flavour and texture of the final product is greatly influenced by the particular micro-organisms used in the process and the length of time they are fermented. Such products may be liquid or semi-solid and can be flavoured with artificial flavourings, fruit pieces, etc. Common types of fermented milks are described in Table 4.

Miscellaneous milk-based products

A wide variety of other products derived from milk do not fall in any of the pre-vious categories. These include creams, milk-based sweets which are very important in Asia, dried milk protein or casein, alcoholic vodka-like beverages, body lotions and soaps.

Ice-cream

Ice-cream is a major milk-based product but it is considered to be beyond the scope of this source book. While large amounts of ice-cream are produced at small-scale levels around the world, it is very difficult to control its microbiological safety and the product carries a very substantial health risk if not produced and distributed under strict conditions. For these reasons, the small-scale manufacture of ice-cream is not recommended in most situations. Readers considering ice-cream manufacture should contact local specialist advisers.

2
Traditional methods and products

MILK PROCESSING is an important activity in many developing countries for many reasons, particularly at the household level. The products can provide income, be consumed in the home, find use in rituals and form an important dietary source, especially for vegetarians. The traditional methods of processing that have evolved over many years of dairy farming take into account local factors such as climatic conditions, indigenous knowledge, availability of resources and the level of hygiene in the kitchen. The resulting products are, to a very large extent, intrinsically safe for local use. Great care is needed in any attempt to replicate the manufacture of a traditional dairy product in another area, since differences in climate, knowledge and experience may result in a product that is unsafe for consumption.

Traditional technologies serve several major functions:

o conserving milk;
o increasing the market value of milk;
o providing improved food security in the home;
o generating income;
o reducing the volume and so lowering transport costs.

Because of the high temperature and humidity in the tropics, farmers have developed an appropriate technology for keeping milk longer without refrigeration facilities. Milk is allowed to sour naturally, which prevents the growth of harmful micro-organisms. Thus, most traditional dairy products start from soured milk. In some countries, such as India, milk is boiled down to remove most of the water and produce a concentrated and more stable product.

During the time of peak production, surpluses may occur and create problems, especially when the market within a small community is limited. The farmer may also not have income from milk during the lean months. To cope with seasonality, milk products are dried, salted, smoked or soaked in salted whey to preserve them. In many cases however, the unhygienic conditions of processing make prolonged storage difficult and the product spoils rapidly.

In general, sanitation and hygiene in household milk processing is poor. Owing to the scarcity of clean water, washing of udders, milk cans and other utensils is inadequate. In some places in Africa, because of the scarcity of water, containers are smoked prior to milking and this is said to give a certain degree of sterilization aside from imparting a smoky flavour to the milk. Alternatively, containers are exposed to the heat of the sun.

These methods are less effective than boiling water or bleach. The quantities of milk processed by most traditional pastoralists are small, perhaps only a few litres per household. The equipment used is therefore very simple and of the type commonly found in the kitchen. The same containers are often used for milking and for fermentation.

Despite the small quantities involved, however, processing milk increases its value. Selling products like cheese and sweets will give the producer a higher return than liquid milk.

Cheeses

The cheesemaking traditions that have developed around the world vary a great

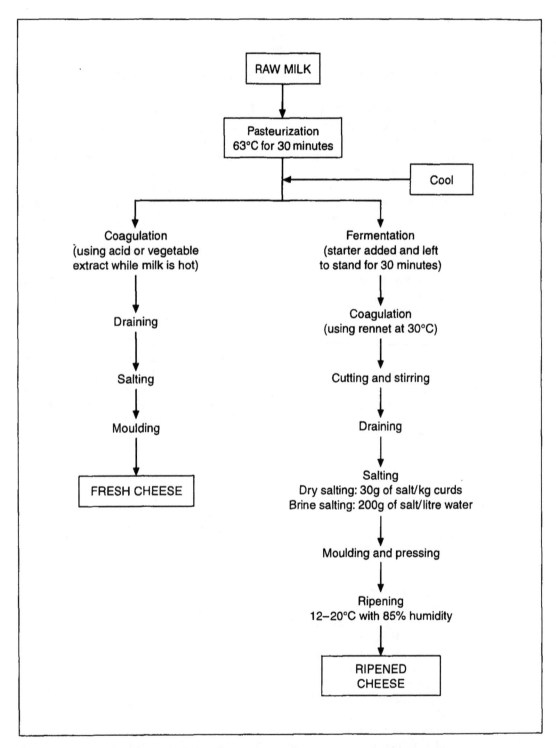

Figure 1. General method of cheesemaking

deal. Figure 1 shows the basic common steps in cheese production. The strongest traditions exist in cool highland areas which are ideal for raising milk-producing animals and in arid areas with enough grazing for sheep and goats. There is very little tradition of dairying and milk processing in hot, humid tropical areas. Some countries, for example those in Southern and Eastern Africa, have no tradition of cheese production.

The type of cheese produced varies considerably from one locality to another because the techniques are highly dependent on local conditions, milk quality, skills and the availability of ingredients. A summary of some common types of cheese is shown in Table 6 on pages 12 and 13.

The first step in the cheesemaking process may involve heating the milk over a fire. In some cases the milk is brought to boiling point, in others simply warmed to about 50°C. Whether or not the milk is heated, and to what temperature, will have a considerable effect on the characteristics, microbiology and flavour of the final cheese. If heated, the milk is generally cooled before further processing.

If cheese is made from raw unheated milk there is a common practice of allowing the milk to stand for a day or two to sour naturally in order to increase its acidity. This is important in curdling the milk in cheesemaking.

The next step is to add the coagulant, which causes the curd to separate. A wide range of traditional coagulants find use in traditional cheese production including plant extracts, sour whey, lime juice, vinegar, and home-made rennet. Home-made rennet is obtained from pieces of lamb, calf or kid stomach. The use of cow-based rennet, it should be noted, would not be permissible for Hindus. The pieces of stomach may be added directly to the milk, or soaked in brine and a portion of this brine – containing the enzymes – added to the milk. Increasingly nowadays, commercially produced rennet is available to traditional cheese producers, particularly in Latin America.

Some common types of traditional milk coagulants are shown in Table 5.

The most common cheeses are of the soft fresh type. This is the simplest method and requires only the minimum equipment but has a shorter shelf-life.

Table 5. Types of traditional milk coagulants

Coagulant	Product/country	Rates used
Bryophylum stems	*Wagashi*/Africa	4 stems per litre of milk
Calotropis procera	*Wara*/Benin	2–8 leaves per litre of milk
	Wagassirou/Nigeria	
Bromelin from pineapple or papain from papaya	*Tahu susu atau dadih*/Indonesia	Not indicated
Lactic acid (chemical form sour whey)	*Channa*/India	2.0–2.5g per litre of milk 1 part for every 4 parts of milk
Citric acid or lime juice	*Paneer*/India	1.0–1.5% of milk
Rennet: tablet, powder or liquid	Use is widespread all over the world	1 tablet/100 litres 1 tsp/40 litres; 20–30ml/ 100 litres
Vinegar	*Kesong puti*/Philippines	25ml/litre

Table 6. Summary of features and processing methods of some cheeses

Product (country)	Type	Raw material	Processing method				Packaging/ storage	Shelf-life
			Heat treatment	Coagulation	Curd treatment			
Ayib (Ethiopia)	Fresh, crumbly, sour curd	Sour whole milk and butter oil	40°C	Natural souring	Drained and packed	→	Kept in bowl or pot at room temperature	One week
Gibbna (Sudan)	Soft, slightly sour and salty	Whole milk (cow, sheep, goat)	None	Natural souring and rennet	Drained, moulded, pressed and cut into blocks	→	Soaked in brine or salted whey	200 days
Wagashi (W. Africa)	Soft, slightly sour and salty	Whole cow milk	Boiled 3–5 min.	Juice extract or stems of bryophylum	Strained, formed into balls and salted	→	Soaked in 25% brine	14 days
							Without brine	3 days
Wara (Benin and Nigeria)	Fresh soft curd, slightly sour and salty	Whole milk (cow or goat)	45–50°C	Juice extract of Calotropis procera	Drained, moulded, salted and dyed (red sorghum)	→	Room temperature. May be salted, smoked or dried	One month
Channa (Bangladesh, India and Nepal)	Soft curd, base material for milk sweets	Cow or buffalo milk	Boiled	Lactic acid or sour whey	Strained through cheesecloth	→	Wrapped in vegetable parchment and kept at room temperature	2–3 days
						→	Cold storage at 7°C	12 days
Serkham (Nepal and Bhutan)	Fresh or dried, slightly sour	Whole milk (cow, yak, buffalo)	Boiled	Natural souring or sour whey	Churned to remove butter, boiled, drained and curd is formed into ball	→	May be pressed and sun-dried and kept in bamboo baskets	2 weeks
Quesillo (Bolivia, Chile, Ecuador)	Fresh, unripened cheese, slightly sour and salty	Whole or partly skimmed cow milk or mixture of cow/goat/sheep milks	None	Rennet	Cut, stirred and partly drained, moulded and slightly pressed	→	Wrapped in plastic bags and kept at room temperature	2–4 days

Product (country)	Type	Raw material	Processing method				Shelf-life
			Heat treatment	Coagulation	Curd treatment	Packaging/storage	
Queso andino (Peru and Ecuador)	Ripened, semi-hard	Whole cow milk	65°C for 15 minutes	Starter and rennet	Cut, drained, pressed and brine-salted	→ 14 days at 13–15°C → Cool storage	2 months
Halloumi (Cyprus and Africa)	White, slightly sour, ripened, semi-hard	Sheep or goat milk	32°C	Rennet	Curd is cut, heated, drained and pressed, then heated in whey and drained, salted.	→ 30 days in brine → Sealed in containers in brine	3–12 months
Braided cheese (Sudan)	Semi-hard, slightly sour and salty	Whole milk (cow, goat or sheep)	30–40°C	Rennet	Drained on cheesecloth, salt and black cumin added, heated, cut into strips and braided	→ None → Kept in tins with brine	2 weeks
Awshari (Iraq)	Hard, ripened, peppery and sour	Sheep or goat milk	None	Home-made rennet (lamb stomach in 5% spiced brine)	Cut, salted, heated, drained and pressed	→ 9 weeks salted in sheep or goat skin → Dry animal skin	6 months
Djamid (Jordan)	Hard, dried, unripened	Sheep or goat milk	40–65°C	Natural souring	Strained, pressed, formed into balls and salted	→ 8–15 days sun- or air-dried → Earthenware or glass jars	6–12 months
Tulim peyneri (Turkey)	Hard, ripened	Whole milk (sheep, goat, buffalo)	None	Starter and rennet	Cut, heated, drained, salted and pressed	→ 90–120 days → Wrapped in animal skin or stomach	6 months or more
Goya (Argentina and Uruguay)	Hard, ripened and slightly salty	Whole cow milk	72°C for 15 seconds	Sour whey and rennet	Cut, cooked, moulded, pressed and brine-salted for 6 days	→ 90 days at 14–16°C 80–85% relative humidity → Cool storage	3 months or more
Takammart (Algeria)	Very hard, unripened	Goat milk	None	Rennet (kid's abomasum)	Drained, dried under the sun for 2–3 days	→ None → Wrapped in animal skin	6–12 months

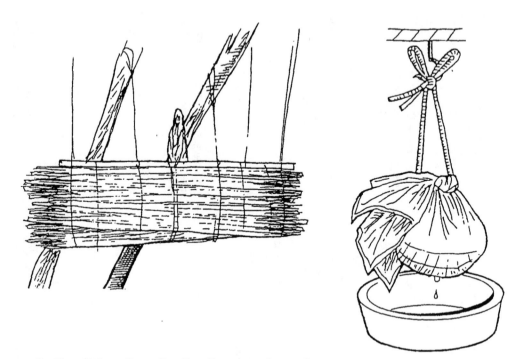

Figure 2. Traditional methods of separating whey

After coagulation, the soft curd has to be separated from the whey. Two common methods, hanging in a piece of cloth or in a straw mat, are shown in Figure 2.

Owing to its high moisture content, the shelf-life of soft cheese is very short. For this reason, it is a common practice to mix up to 10 per cent of salt with the curd to make the cheese last longer and to improve its flavour. The salt acts as a preservative by making moisture unavailable for use by micro-organisms. Alternatively, the curd is submerged in containers of whey to which salt has been added. In other cases the curd is sun-dried (see Figure 3).

In order to produce a cheese with a longer shelf-life, the moisture content has to be reduced by squeezing out more whey than is possible by simple draining. The curd is placed in simple wooden moulds and pressed. A range of different press designs using the weight of stones, levers or twisted ropes can be used and typical examples are shown in Figure 4. This results in semi-hard and hard cheeses which are produced in Latin America, the Middle East and North Africa. Few of these traditional cheeses are ripened by ageing. Ripening, if done, is short and mainly accomplished in village milk centres but rarely at household level because of the necessity for refrigeration facilities and the fact that the producers wish to gain income as quickly as possible. In addition, the flavour and texture of ripened cheeses are often not liked in societies which are most accustomed to soft cheeses.

Butters

Although butter is produced traditionally, it is rarely used as table butter. More commonly it is regarded as a cooking fat, although some unusual uses exist. For example, in Tibet it is added to salted tea. Other uses are non-food-related, such as

Figure 3. Traditional ways of sun-drying cheese

 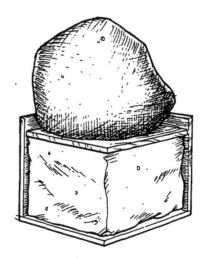

Figure 4. Some examples of traditional moulds and cheese presses

body lotions to ward off the effects of extreme cold in, for example, Nepal.

The production of butter involves the churning or agitation of sour milk or cream so that the fat forms a semi-solid mass. This is removed from the remaining liquid, the buttermilk, and then worked and pressed to remove as much buttermilk as possible. The typical production steps are shown in Figure 5.

Traditionally, butter is produced from sour milk for several good reasons. First, there is a preference for the slightly sour flavour. Secondly, the conditions under which the milk is produced combined with warm temperatures and the lack of refrigeration means that the milk sours and curdles fast. It should be noted that under the typical hygienic conditions in a home, the souring of milk prevents the growth of possible pathogenic micro-organisms.

Finally, butter can be prepared much more quickly from sour milk than from cream, due to its lower viscosity and, when small amounts are being prepared, churning whole milk is more manageable than churning cream. Traditional butter is not always made from sour milk, however. In the Middle East and some parts of North Africa, for example, the cream is separated and collected over a few days or until a sufficient quantity is saved from processing. This holding period allows the cream to sour, giving the same advantages as mentioned above.

Churning

Traditional butter churns are made from local materials, and usually hold small quantities of milk. Some African pastoralists make butter by filling a closed gourd, calabash or clay pot half-full of sour milk. The 3–5 litre capacity vessel is rocked back and forth on a woman's lap or on the ground, on top of a small cushion. Another method is to suspend the vessel from a

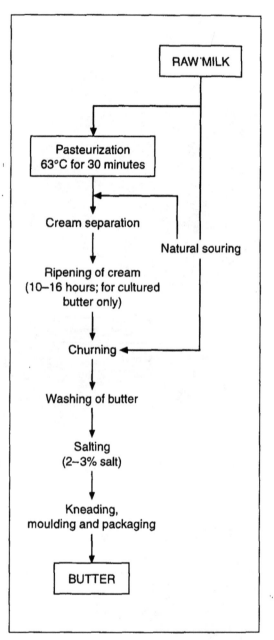

Figure 5. Traditional production of butter

wooden post or tripod and swing it to and fro until butter grains appear. For smaller vessels, churning is done by raising or shaking the containers occasionally, removing the cover to release the air inside.

Other pastoralists in Africa commonly use goat or sheep skins filled up to two-thirds of their capacity. Air is blown into the skin to expand it, allowing more room for the milk to move during churning. The skin is hung between several poles and shaken until butter appears. This method is also widely used in the Middle East. In Somalia, some ethnic groups make butter by pouring milk into skin bags which they sling on their shoulder while walking and push with an elbow to swing to and fro.

In Nepal, cylindrical wooden churns, with piston-type paddles which are pulled up and down, are traditionally used. In

Figure 6. Traditional methods of churning butter using calabashes and clay pots

Latin America, traditional small-scale buttermaking is based on the churning technology brought by the Spaniards using the barrel-type churn.

Freshly made butter still contains a lot of water which has to be pressed out to make the butter more stable. Traditionally this is done with the hands or flat pieces of wood. Also, in some cultures salt is added, which increases the shelf-life.

The most common traditional types of packaging used for butter are earthenware pots, gourds and wooden bowls. In

Figure 7. Churning butter using a goat or sheep skin

Figure 8. Piston-type wooden churn

some countries, such as Nigeria, the butter is formed into balls and stored in earthenware pots filled with buttermilk.

Ghee

Fresh butter is difficult to store and quickly becomes rancid, particularly in tropical climates. The butter is boiled in a large shallow pan to reduce its water content further, a process which destroys micro-organisms and enzymes, such as lipase, and thus makes it much more stable. Such products are widely known as ghee or clarified butter and are very popular in many tropical countries. Ghee has a superior keeping quality, mainly because of its low moisture content (about 1 per cent) and the heating process destroys most of the spoilage micro-organisms and enzymes. A good ghee will last for 6–12

months at room temperature without becoming rancid. It has many uses such as frying oil, shortening and as a general cooking ingredient.

In Southern and Eastern Africa, an intermediate product between ghee and butter is made by heating butter at 40°C, giving a substance with about 10 per cent moisture. This is said to keep for six months at room temperature.

Fermented milks

Soured fermented milks are popular in many tropical countries and are widely consumed as refreshing summer drinks, desserts or snack items. The consistency of the final product depends on the type of milk used, the process and time. In India

Table 7. Summary of features and processing methods of some traditional butters

Product (country)	Type/use	Raw material	Processing method			Packaging/ storage	Shelf-life
			Heat treatment	Fermentation	Cream treatment		
Gibde (Chad)	Unwashed butter for cooking and baby food	Whole cow milk	None	Natural souring	Shaken in a gourd for 1–2 hours	Kept in a calabash in a cool dry place	3–4 weeks
Ghee (Indian sub-continent, Middle East and Africa)	Clarified butter	Milk from various animals	None	Natural souring	Separated, may or may not be churned, heated to evaporate moisture	Kept in earthenware pots, metal or glass containers at room temperature	One year
Keshda mosakhana (Egypt)	Cylindrical shaped heated fresh cream for desserts	Buffalo milk	Boiled for 30 minutes	None	Left to stand overnight and skimmed	Placed in cylindrical containers and kept in cool dry place	One week
Shmen (Algeria, Mali and Niger)	Clarified butter mainly for cooking	Camel milk	None	Natural souring for 12–24 hours	Churned in a goat skin, butter is collected and boiled to evaporate	Kept in covered containers at room temperature	6 months or more

and neighbouring countries, yoghurt is an important ingredient in many culinary dishes.

The general method of processing, which is shown in Figure 9, usually starts with filtration of the raw milk into vessels. The milk is left to sour naturally for 24–28 hours depending on the temperature. In some countries the milk is heated and a small amount of the previous day's product, which already contains the fermenting micro-organisms or 'starter culture', is added.

The starter micro-organisms used in traditional processing occur naturally in the milk, air and on surfaces on containers. There are several different types of starter, each producing a final product with a characteristic taste, smell and texture. The most common starters belong to a group of micro-organisms known as *Lactobacillus* which occur in milk. Other starters include *Streptococcus* and certain yeasts. Since yeasts produce alcohol and carbon dioxide as they grow, products using these starters, such as *kefir* and *airag*, are slightly fizzy and alcoholic. In many natural fermentations a mixture of starter micro-organisms are involved in the process.

After fermentation the product is ready for direct consumption. However, other ingredients are sometimes added to make the product more tasty and attractive, such as natural food colours, flavours and food pieces.

The thickness of yoghurts and soured milks can be modified according to local preferences. In Ethiopia, it is a common practice to siphon off the whey after the milk has curdled and add new milk to the batch. This is repeated until the container is filled with curds. The curd is then consumed or stored in the same container. In the Middle East, yoghurt is drained through a cheesecloth until the desired consistency is reached. Some salt, sugar

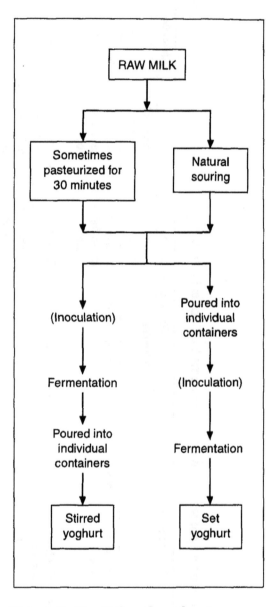

Figure 9. Traditional yoghurt production

or spices may be added to the drained mass. A watery yoghurt is made by diluting it with water and adding either salt or sugar to taste. This is called *lassi* in India, and is a popular drink which is produced commercially. When sour milk is used to make butter, the remaining buttermilk is also widely consumed as a drink, sometimes after fermentation.

The most important piece of equipment used in traditional fermented milk processing is the milk vessel. Most vessels are made from materials such as gourds, clay, wood and, rarely, tin and copper.

The warm temperature of the tropics makes fermentation possible without the use of special equipment such as incubators, although it takes a day or more. In the Middle East where the nights are cold, containers are wrapped with woollen sheets to keep a constant temperature. Another practice is to keep the milk container near the stove while cooking is going on.

Figure 10. Removing the whey from curdled milk through a wooden straw

Figure 11. Examples of traditional milk containers

Table 8. Summary of features and processing methods of some traditional fermented milk products

Product (country)	Type	Raw material	Processing method				Shelf-life
			Heat treatment	Starter added	Incubation	Packaging/ storage	
Yoghurt (Asia, Africa and Latin America)	Sour milk	Milk from various animals	None	Natural souring	24–28 hours at room temperature	Consumed immediately	N/A
Chambiko (Malawi)	Concentrated sour milk	Whole milk of cow or zubu	None	Natural souring	3–4 days at room temperature, whey is removed	Kept in calabash at room temperature	One week
Airag (Mongolia)	Sour, slightly alcoholic milk	Mare's milk	65°C for 30 minutes	Airag starter	10–12 hours at 18–20°C	Glass jars or other containers at room temperature	One week
Dahi (India)	Sour milk	Cow or buffalo milk	Heated to boiling	Previous day's dahi	Overnight	Refrigerated	One week
Mishti doi (India)	Sweetened sour milk	Cow and buffalo milk	Sugar, colour and caramel are boiled with milk	Previous day's product	12–15 hours at 40–45°C	Consumed immediately or refrigerated	One week
Kefir (Russia)	Acidic, effervescent milk	Goat, sheep or cow milk	Pasterurized (85°C for 30 minutes) then cooled to room temperature	Kefir grains (25–30g grains per 500ml milk)	24–48 hours at room temperature (max. 25°C), sieved to removed kefir grains, incubated again 24 hours	Refrigerated	One week

Table 9. Summary of features and processing methods of some miscellaneous milk products

More information on these and other unusual milk products can be found in 'The Technology of Traditional Milk Products in Developing Countries' (FAO, 1990)

Product (country)	Type/description	Outline of method	Storage
Amavuta (Zaire)	Body cream/yellowish, firm but spreadable, rancid odour	Whole cow milk is soured and boiled with pieces of wood or leaves while melted fat is collected into a covered vessel.	Few months
Chak mapuo (Kenya)	Acidified milk/yellowish and lumpy with sharp, sour taste	Whole zebu milk is placed into a vessel, previously rinsed with heifer urine and fermented spontaneously for 2–3 days. Two-day-old heifer urine is added and mixture is churned until butter grains appear.	Several days
Mkango (Kenya)	Thick, grainy dried paste/brown colour with sweet taste	Maize grain is roasted, ground and mixed with whole milk and honey. The mixture is heated, stirring constantly until thick and vessel is covered with embers overnight or until cooked.	2 months at room temperature
Omokora (Kenya)	Slightly acid drink/dark brown and lumpy	Raw milk is boiled and mixed with previously beaten cow blood (4:1). This may be consumed immediately or allowed to ferment.	2 weeks at room temperature
Silmissaffande/ Katare (Burkina Faso)	Traditional soap/soft and spreadable with no odour	Milk cream is boiled, potash and millet flour are added, stirring continuously until mixture is thick. The paste is kneaded and formed into spheres.	Kept in calabash at room temperature for an indefinite period
Eezgii (Mongolia)	Milk protein-based product/yellowish, dry and lumpy with sweet, milky taste	Curdled milk is boiled until the whey is absorbed into the curds. Heating is continued till it is golden brown in colour. The final product is sun-dried.	6 months at room temperature
Khoa (India, Nepal, Bhutan, Pakistan)	Concentrated whole-milk paste/white to yellowish, slightly oily or granular	Cow or buffalo milk is heated with constant stirring until milk thickens and forms a semi-solid mass; formed into pats or made into sweets.	2 weeks in refrigeration
Kulfi (India)	Milk-based ice-cream/flavoured with chocolate, groundnuts or fruit pulp	Raw milk and sugar are boiled until mixture is half its original volume; indigenous cream, nuts and flavours added, mixed and poured into moulds. This is frozen in a large earthenware vessel 1:1 mixture of ice and salt.	Consumed immediately

(continues on page 24)

Table 9. *Continued*

Product (country)	Type/description	Outline of method	Storage
Leche flan (Philippines)	Dessert delicacy/jelly-like, homogeneous with sweet taste	Moulds are lined with caramelized sugar and set aside; whole milk is mixed with condensed milk and egg yolks, strained and poured into moulds and cooked in double boiler until firm.	3–5 days at room temperature; 2–3 weeks in refrigeration
Muktaghar monda (Bangladesh)	Dried delicacy/white to yellowish with sour and spicy taste	Whole milk is boiled until proteins coagulate; whey is drained and precipitate is ground by hand; sugar and spices are added and the mixture is cooled.	3–7 days at room temperature
Orom (Mongolia)	Concentrated milk/yellowish with homogeneous texture	Whole milk is heated and allowed to cool, and the film which forms on the surface is collected. This is done repeatedly until no more milk is left.	30 days in a cool place
Churpi (Nepal, Bhutan)	Precipitated protein/very hard and rubbery	Buttermilk is warmed until flakes are formed and it takes a yellow-greenish colour; the curd is strained, moulded, pressed with stone and cut into small pieces. These are threaded on a string and sun-dried or placed near the stove.	Several years
Serkahm (Nepal, Bhutan)	Milk casein/light green coarse powder with acid taste	Yak or chowri buttermilk is heated until proteins precipitate and it takes a yellow-greenish colour; the precipitate is drained, squeezed by hand, formed into long strips or flattened and dried under the sun.	Several years
Peda/Gundpak (India, Nepal)	Sweet delicacy made from *khoa*/whitish to yellow with coarse texture	*Khoa* and sugar are mixed and gently heated until firm balls are formed; nuts and flavours are added and shaped as desired; wrapped in greaseproof paper and packed in cartons.	2 weeks
Cola de mono (Chile)	Slightly alcoholic beverage/clear brown colour with pleasant flavour	Whole or partly skimmed milk is mixed with an alcoholic drink, sugar and coffee.	Consumed immediately

Miscellaneous milk products

A wide range of miscellaneous milk products is made in developing countries in order to use seasonal surpluses, reduce transportation and handling problems, and to improve the nutritional and eating qualities of staple foods such as maize and sorghum. Most of the products are made for human consumption but some are used for cosmetic purposes.

In most cases, these products are prepared mainly for household consumption. Notable exceptions are the heat coagulated products (*khoa* and *channa*) of India and neighbouring countries which are produced commercially as sweetmeats.

In a general book of this type it is not possible to describe the large number of miscellaneous products based on milk. The table on pages 23 and 24, however, is included to offer some examples.

3
Improving milk processing technologies

IMPROVEMENTS that can be made in dairy production do not depend greatly on changing the basic steps in the processes which have been outlined in the flow diagrams (Figures 1, 5 and 9) for each product. Rather, they involve changing the conditions and the way in which the steps are carried out. In this chapter, advice is given for improvements which can be made both at household and at commercial level. For commercial production, a purpose-built building is generally required.

As has been described, traditional dairy production depends upon the natural or forced souring of milk so that safe products can be made under the hygienic condition of a typical kitchen. Improvements at the household level, therefore, do not aim to create non-traditional products but simply to improve the final quality. When moving to commercial production, particularly when non-traditional dairy foods are produced, the process does not normally use soured milk but fresh milk. This means that safe products have to rely totally on the quality of the incoming raw milk and the hygienic conditions in the processing plant. Essentially, the changes and improvements seen as producers move from domestic to commercial production involve:

o the more widespread use of fresh milk rather than soured milk as a starting material;
o a greater attention to sanitation and hygiene;
o including quality control in the whole process and producing a standard product;
o the increasing use of refrigeration, pasteurization and rapid cooling;

o increasing use of specially designed equipment that can be kept spotlessly clean, with stainless steel becoming more common as scale increases;
o production in purpose-built building;
o in the production of cheeses and yoghurts, the necessity of using special starters and cultures;
o the use of modern packaging materials, presentation and marketing.

Traditional milk processing in developing countries is characterized by the small volumes of milk treated per household, the level of sanitation and hygiene found in the home and the scarcity of resources such as equipment, fuel, clean water and, for many women, time. Despite these limitations, rural householders have developed processes and techniques that take account of existing conditions and can produce safe, acceptable products. These are adapted according to locally available resources, suitability in the diet, and an understanding of the marketing system which is usually very local. Many examples of the way that traditional milk processing systems overcome local constraints have been described in Chapter 2.

Some improvements can, however, be made to traditional household technologies at comparatively low cost. These improvements must be directed by the circumstances and needs of the users. The introduction of improved practices should not replace the time-tested, safe, traditional methods unless it is clear that the producers have both the knowledge and capacity to implement them properly. For example, heat treatment appears, at first sight, a simple way to improve micro-

biological quality. In fact, it is never prac-
tised in many developing countries as the
products rely on the growth of natural
acid-forming organisms which prevent the
growth of harmful bacteria. Improvements
that can be made mainly involve the use of
labour-saving devices and the reduction of
the level of contamination by micro-
organisms, flies, etc. Such improvements
are described in the following sections on
cheese, butter and fermented milks.

When processors move from production
at the household level, for home or very
local consumption, to producing larger
quantities of milk commodities that can
be distributed over a wider area, they
take on considerable responsibility to
their customers. For example, a low-salt
cream cheese produced and safely consumed in a cool mountainous area will
very likely cause food poisoning if marketed in a nearby lowland tropical region.

Thus, when handling larger quantities
of milk (30 litres or more per day), sanitation and hygiene during milk handling
and processing become extremely important and quality control testing may become essential.

When considering improvements that
involve commercial production, the all-
important marketing aspects must receive
serious attention. A marketing strategy
will need to be developed as well as packaging, distribution and advertising
systems.

As some of the case studies show, dairy
processing can be improved by sharing traditional knowledge and current practices
between communities and countries. In
some cases where centralized milk collection takes place, for example co-operatives,
it may be appropriate to use more modern
hygienic processing techniques.

The following section on milk handling,
hygiene and quality aspects is important
as it will help those assisting milk producers to give more informed advice.

Nevertheless, before making firm recom-
mendations, advice should be sought from
specialists in the area.

Sanitation and hygiene

Good quality products are made from
good quality raw materials. In the case of
dairy products, this means fresh, pure
and clean milk from healthy animals. The
milk should be free from odours and
taints that could affect the quality of
finished products. To ensure the cleanliness of milk, a high level of sanitation
should be enforced during milking and
subsequent handling.

By its very nature, milk carries a
higher public safety risk than many other
foods, so the level of cleanliness is vital.
Everything should be kept as clean as
possible to keep the level of contamination at its lowest, with good sanitation
practices observed from the farm to the
processing area.

On the farm:

o the milking premises should be kept
clean, removing all dirt which attracts
insects, rodents and other pests;
o milk containers and other dairy utensils should be thoroughly washed and
disinfected before and after use;
o udders should be cleaned with a clean,
dry cloth and only washed and dried if
very dirty;
o the animal should be checked periodi-
cally for diseases and the milk should
be tested for mastitis (a testing kit for
this is available from a local veterinary
supplier);
o the milkers should observe proper personal hygiene: frequent hand-washing,
keeping hair covered and refraining
from handling milk if they have any infection or disease;

o the milk should be covered and kept as cool as possible while being transported to the processing area in the shortest time possible.

In the processing plant:

o the incoming raw milk should be tested for microbiological quality, fat content and adulteration as soon as it is received;
o milk should be pasteurized and cooled as soon as possible;
o raw milk should be in a separate room from pasteurized milk to reduce cross-contamination;
o the processing area should always be kept clean and tidy, giving special attention to all surfaces and storage areas;
o the premises should be kept free from rodents, flies and other pests;
o all equipment and utensils should be washed and disinfected very well and, where applicable, sterilized;
o equipment should be smooth, unscratched and designed for easy, efficient cleaning;
o milk handlers should wear clean clothes, caps and observe proper hygiene at all times.

After cleaning equipment and utensils, sterilizing will further ensure safety and sanitation. This can be done by:

o scalding with hot water, 100°C for 10 minutes or 80°C for 30 minutes;
o rinsing in hypochlorite solution (household bleach – 2 tbsp for every 4.5 litres of water).

If any of the above methods are not possible, washing and subsequent drying in the sun will help. It is not, however, a substitute for the above methods.

Working surfaces should be disinfected by wiping with bleach after making sure they have been thoroughly cleaned.

Heat treatment

The process of heating milk to a temperature that is sufficiently high to destroy harmful micro-organisms without destroying the sensory and nutritional qualities of the milk is called pasteurization. Pasteurization performs several functions in dairy processing:

o improves the safety of the milk;
o allows added starter cultures to produce the desired results by reducing competition from other micro-organisms;
o prolongs the shelf-life of the product;
o allows the production of a more standard product with less variation;
o destroys the rancidity-producing enzyme, lipase.

There are several methods of heat treatment to suit the purposes for which the milk is to be used, the availability of resources and the scale of processing. Ultra-high temperature sterilization (UHT) involves very expensive equipment and is only viable at the very large scale.

After pasteurization, rapid cooling stops the loss of sensory qualities and the nutritional value of milk. Ideally, it should be cooled to 4–10°C but this is particularly difficult without refrigeration. On a small scale, an alternative is to use a cold water bath, immersing the kettle with the warm milk in a big pan of cold running water. The milk should be stirred to hasten cooling. The use of ice, if available, will help in cooling the water sufficiently.

Testing milk quality

Quality control testing is important to protect the consumer and produce a

Table 10. Methods of heat treatment

Type	Temperature	Time	Product made from milk
Low temperature (conventional)	63°C	30 min.	Fresh milk, cheese
High temperature short time (HTST)	72°C	15 sec.	Yoghurt, butter, cheese
Ultra-high temperature (UHT)	135–150°C	2 to 4 sec.	Sterilized milk

consistently high standard of finished product. In most countries, regulations exist which insist on quality control testing to protect the customers.

The level and amount of testing will vary from country to country and advice should be sought from relevant local authorities. Increasingly nowadays, more and more countries require all food products sold commercially to be tested for quality, including traditional products.

Testing and controls (sensory, microbiological, physical and chemical) are necessary at three stages:

o raw milk testing to establish the freshness, purity and hygienic quality of milk;
o processing controls to ensure that certain key steps contribute to the desired quality of the finished product;
o finished product testing to ensure that the product meets established quality standards.

Sensory analysis

These are methods of measuring quality by the appearance, flavour and odour characteristics of food products.

o Normal milk has a white to yellowish colour and is slightly more viscous than water. The appearance of abnormalities such as discoloration, lumps or a high viscosity makes the milk unacceptable.
o Milk should have a bland, slightly sweet taste and a pleasant smell. Some-

times, milk is contaminated by exposure to strong odours which it readily absorbs.

Two simple tests are commonly used. In the Finger Test, which is widely used in India, a small amount of milk is placed in a saucer. A finger is put in and slowly drawn out. If a string or thread of milk is seen on the finger end, the milk is not suitable. In the California Test, some washing-up liquid is mixed with some milk. If the milk remains liquid it is good to use.

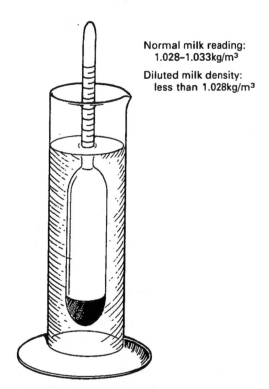

Normal milk reading:
1.028–1.033kg/m³

Diluted milk density:
less than 1.028kg/m³

Figure 12. Using a lacto-densimeter

Table 11. Grading system for Methylene Blue Test

White colour reached	Bacterial level	Milk quality
Within 20 minutes	Very high	Bad
Less than 2 hours	High	Poor
Less than 5 hours	Medium	Good
After 5 hours	Low	Excellent

Source: Smeets and Hameleers, 1991

Physical and chemical tests

The most commonly applied tests are the measurement of density and fat content. They are used to determine if the milk has been watered down or if any fat has been skimmed off. Although the tests are simple, training is essential. Density is checked using a lacto-densimeter as shown in Figure 12.

Fat content is checked by the Gerber Test, which is simple but requires more training than density testing. Fat testing is essential if milk standardization (described in the next section, on improvements to cheesemaking) is being considered.

Microbiological tests

These tests measure the hygienic quality of milk and should be used as a basis for the acceptance or rejection of raw milk. They can help in deciding what further treatment the milk might need. The quality of the raw milk dictates what kinds of final product can be made. For example, a milk with a slightly poor microbiological quality could be acceptable for manufacturing boiled milk sweets but not for cheese. A detailed discussion of microbiological testing methods is beyond the scope of this source book and it is recommended that expert advice be sought.

The Methylene Blue Test is a widely used and simple test. Micro-organisms make use of the oxygen present in milk as they grow and the Methylene Blue Test measures how quickly oxygen is being used up. This determines how many micro-organisms are present.

Method: A thoroughly mixed sample of milk (20ml) is placed in a test tube and 0.5ml of dye solution (0.0075% methylene blue) is added. The dye and milk are mixed by inverting the closed tubes. The test tubes are kept in a water bath at 36–38°C and protected against light. The length of time it takes for the dye to fade is recorded and compared to the times shown in Table 11.

Local regulations should be consulted regarding rejection limits.

Improvements to cheesemaking

Simple improvements at the household level

Provided that water of reasonable quality is available, perhaps the most dramatic improvement that could be made by a household cheesemaker is to use a few drops of household bleach in all water used to clean the animal before milking, and to wash utensils, work surfaces and hands.

When soft cheeses are being produced it is far better to drain them in squares of

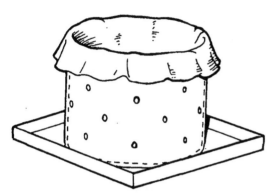

Figure 13. Improved draining of whey

white muslin cheesecloth that are washed and sterilized by boiling after every use. The cheesecloth can also be used to line the moulds as shown in Figure 13. In addition, covering the draining curd with, for example, plastic sheet will keep out flies and other insects, so reducing contamination and losses of product from spoilage.

When making sun-dried cheese or cheese-like products, simply covering the product with muslin or using a small solar drier will substantially reduce contamination by dust and insects.

Semi-hard cheeses can be protected by brushing the outer surface with a salt brine every two days for a week. In the second week, continue brushing using water or whey. Only soft brushes should be used.

Finally, the home producer can improve her product with better protection from packaging. Dipping in hot food-grade wax gives an outer protective coating. If waxing is not possible, wrapping in greaseproof paper will help to keep the product clean.

Improvements involved in small-scale commercial production

When commercial cheese production is planned, a building will be required. Ideally the building should:

o be centrally placed in the milk producing area;
o be near a supply of clean water;
o be sited in a cool, well-ventilated place.

The internal walls of the plant should be rendered with cement to allow easy cleaning, have a sloping concrete floor that allows water to drain away and have windows covered with fly-proof mesh for good ventilation. If ripened cheeses are to be produced, a ripening cellar will need to be constructed partly below ground, in order to maintain cool, humid conditions.

Testing and standardizing

Normally milk from each supplier is tested at least for its density to detect any abnormalities, particularly for added water. At higher production levels, cheese producers 'standardize' the milk. Standardization is a step which involves removing part of the cream to produce milk with a standard fat content for cheese manufacture. It has the advantage that butter can then be made from the cream, so increasing profits.

Pasteurization

After testing, the milk is filtered. It is recommended that the milk should next be pasteurized as described earlier, to eliminate undesirable bacteria which cause defects in the cheese. It is not advisable to boil the milk as this will affect both flavour and nutrients. Intense heat treatment also results in reduced curd formation and gives a bitter taste to cheese when it is ripened (Ebing & Rutgers, 1991). While unpasteurized milk produces a better flavoured cheese and is still traditionally used in some countries, its handling requires a much better degree of hygiene and quality control. In most situations, therefore, the manufacture of

Figure 14. Small-scale production unit suitable for handling 100–500 litres of milk per day

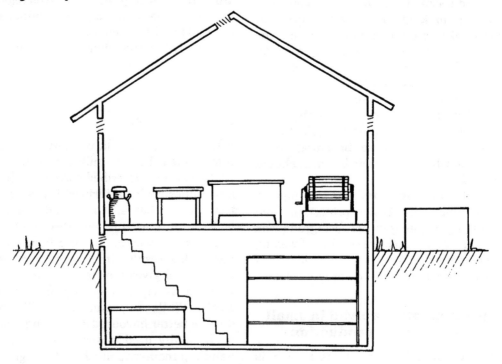

Figure 15. Section of building showing underground ripening room

unpasteurized milk cheeses is not recommended. Using conventional low-temperature pasteurization will destroy undesirable bacteria without greatly affecting cheese quality.

If pasteurization is performed in an ordinary pan over a fire, great care and constant stirring are essential to prevent scorching or overheating the milk. A dairy thermometer is essential although, in its absence, producers soon learn to judge the milk temperature by experience, with surprising accuracy. The use of a double saucepan helps avoid any scorching of the milk.

If the temperature goes above 72°C, the curd will be very soft and it will be difficult to make an acid cheese. For the production of acid-coagulated white cheese, the milk must be heated to 82–85°C. The valuable albumin also precipitates and is not lost with the whey.

At a larger scale, double-walled vats are used for pasteurization. A typical gas-heated example is shown in Figure 16. Such vats are very useful as they can also be used to cool the milk by running cold water through the jacket and for the later coagulation and draining steps.

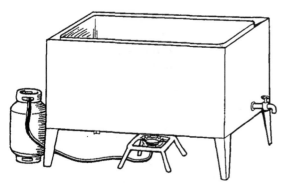

Figure 16. Multi-purpose double-walled vat

Inoculation with starter culture

After the heat treatment and cooling, a starter culture has to be added to ferment the milk, as the heat treatment has destroyed the lactic acid-producing micro-organisms naturally present in the milk. This helps in the flavour development of cheese and also develops the acid necessary for coagulation by rennet. The length of fermentation depends on microbial quality and the temperature used. Starters can be purchased as freeze-dried powders. The preparation and use of starters for both cheeses and yoghurts is described in the FAO 'Village milk processing' guide (1988).

Coagulation

The milk curds are formed, and separated from the whey as the milk is coagulated, by one of the following methods:

o using acid for fresh or unripened cheese: acids are available from natural sources, such as sour whey or lemon juice, or in chemical form, such as citric or lactic acid;

o using rennet for ripened cheese: rennets are prepared from animal, vegetable and microbial sources. They are available in three forms: tablet, powder and liquid.

This is best carried out in a double-jacketed vessel to maintain the desired steady temperature for rennet coagulation. At the small scale, this can be done in a double saucepan and, at the larger scale, in a multi-purpose vat.

Separation of curds

For all cheeses the curds are separated from the whey by draining. The use of simple slanted wooden draining tables greatly helps at this stage.

Figure 17. Wooden cheese-draining table

For fresh cheese, a large portion of the whey is left in the curds, while for ripened cheese, much of the whey is removed by cutting and pressing. After the curd has set, it is first cut using a cheese knife with vertical blades and then with another special knife with horizontal blades. A typical example is shown in Figure 18. This allows an even removal of whey. For small amounts of curd, a long kitchen knife will do. After the curd has been cut, it is drained to remove the whey.

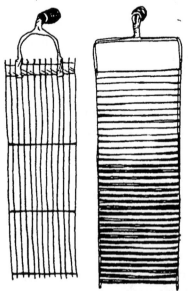

Figure 18. Cheese knives

Salting

After the curds have been cut and drained, salt is added to aid in the further removal of whey, to enhance the flavour of the cheese and to act as a preservative. The salt must be distributed evenly to get uniform ripening. There are two commonly used methods of salting:

o adding dry salt, usually at levels of about 30 grams per kg of curd;
o soaking in brine (20kg salt in 80 litres of water) for about 12 hours at 14–18°C. The cheese should be turned at least once.

If brine salting is used, the soaking time depends on the size of the cheese. A 1kg cheese requires 12–24 hours whereas a 6–8kg cheese needs 3–4 days.

Pressing

Pressing removes more whey from the curd and this is best done by gradually increasing the pressure. For semi-hard and hard cheeses, the use of a cheese press is essential. Presses can be made from wood, metal or plastic but they must ensure that the pressure can be increased gradually.

Cheese moulds can easily be made by cutting plastic drainage pipes into 25cm lengths and then drilling holes in the walls. Bases and lids are made of wooden discs that just fit into the moulds.

Ripening

Ripening is a critical stage where the cheese develops its characteristic flavour, colour, aroma and texture, and loses moisture to improve its keeping quality. For successful ripening, the temperature and humidity in the ripening room should be controlled. This allows certain groups of beneficial micro-organisms to grow

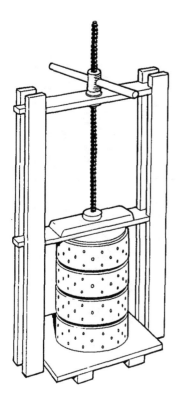

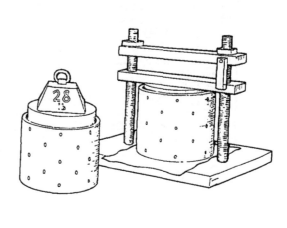

Figure 19. Improved cheese presses

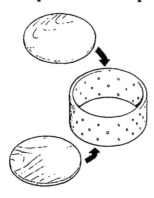

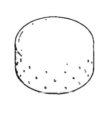

Figure 20. Locally made moulds, bases and lids

while discouraging others, particularly spoilage types. A cool environment (12–20°C) with a high relative humidity (85 per cent) is ideal. The cheeses should be inspected and turned regularly for even ripening.

During ripening, moulds grow on the surface of the cheese and these should be removed by wiping with vinegar or oil. When the necessary conditions for ripening are not available due to an incorrect environment or limited resources, other ways of treating the curd can be used, including drying or smoking. Covering the cheese with food-grade wax gives more protection against butterfat oozing out, excessive drying and hardening.

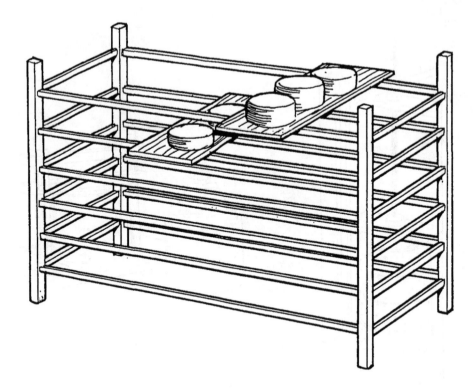

Figure 21. Ripening cheeses on dry, clean wooden planks

Improvements to buttermaking

Possible improvements at the household level

In the same way as for cheese, the use of a few drops of household bleach in all water used to wash utensils will substantially improve the hygiene of the final product.

To reduce the work of churning, butter can be made from cream. Cream separation may be done by leaving the milk to stand for 12–24 hours and skimming off the cream, or by separating the cream in a vessel fitted with a tap as shown in Figure 22. Cream separation from goat's milk is difficult to achieve by standing.

Perhaps the greatest improvement that can be made is to reduce the time and

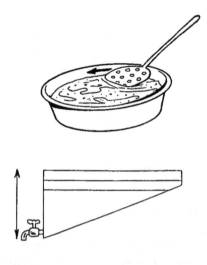

Figure 22. Simple methods of cream separation

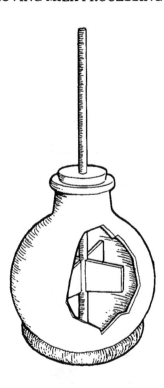

**Figure 23. Improved butter churn
developed in Ethiopia**

amount of work required for churning by
the use of simple mechanical churns. The
case study from Ethiopia (see page 49) describes a very simple churning device
which saves the women producers time
and effort. Figure 23 shows the improved
butter churn.

For a slightly higher production level,
churns of the type shown in Figure 24 are
available with capacities between one and
five litres. Alternatively, an earthenware
piston-type of churn can be used at the
household level.

The quality of product reaching the consumer can be improved by attention to
packaging. Probably the most readily
available packaging is greaseproof paper
and this is a much safer material to use
than plastic bags.

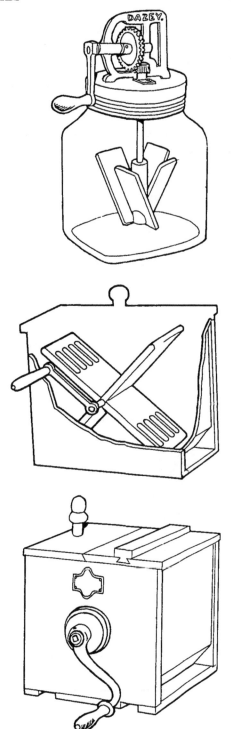

**Figure 24. Other types of improved
butter churns**

Improvements to small-scale commercial butter and ghee production

The main difference between the production of butter at household and commercial levels is the fact that the cream is mechanically separated and there is no need to allow the milk to ripen. Making butter from cream gives a greater yield and is more efficient. The cream is separated by a type of centrifuge called a cream separator which can be manually or electrically operated.

Typical examples of a manual separator with a capacity of approximately 50 litres per hour and a 200-litre-per-hour electric cream separator are shown in Figure 25.

If the local preference is for the flavour of a ripened butter, the cream is either left to stand to develop the characteristic slightly acid flavour, or a starter culture is added.

During churning the fat globules are thrown against a churn surface and coalesce to form butter grains. Good temperature control is important in efficient churning. If the temperature is too low, churning is slow while if it is too high, the butter grains form quickly into large lumps which entrap a lot of whey. For efficient churning, the temperature should be between 8 and 16–20°C.

There are a number of different types of butter churns suitable for small-scale production. Larger sizes of glass churns

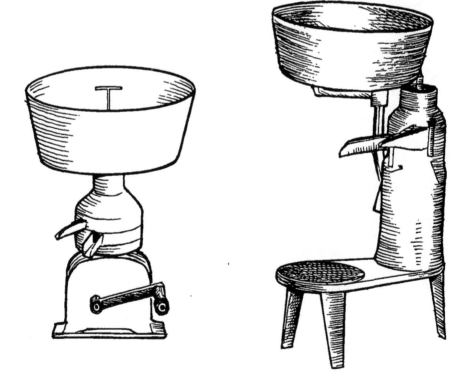

Figure 25. Manual and electric cream separators

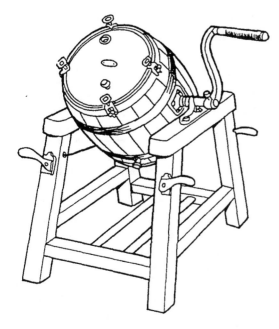

Figure 26. A wooden barrel churn

shown in Figure 24 are commercially available, as are small electric churns and manual or powered wooden rotating barrel churns.

Kneading removes the free water and distributes the trapped moisture evenly throughout the butter, making a smooth mass. At this point, salt at a level of one per cent is added if required. For small quantities, using the hands is sufficient but, with larger quantities, butter rollers and butter pats are very useful.

Good packaging of butter is important as it readily absorbs strong odours. Suitable materials are those which prevent the entry of light such as greaseproof paper and aluminium laminates.

Improvements to fermented milk processing

Possible improvements at the household level

Once again, sanitation can be improved by using household bleach in the washing water. Moving away from clay and gourd fermentation vessels, to plastic or aluminium ones that can be cleaned properly, will also improve product quality.

The other major improvement is to reduce the production time by maintaining the fermenting milk at a reasonably constant temperature. This can be achieved by using a thermos flask or an insulated polystyrene box, both of which are now increasingly available in shops. Initiating the fermentation can be speeded up by

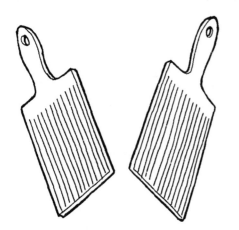

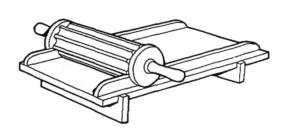

Figure 27. Butter kneading implements

adding a spoonful of the last batch as a starter. This should not, however, be done too many times as there is a danger of the micro-organisms gradually changing and producing unacceptable products. To make a more interesting product, honey, nuts or pieces of fruit can be added to the yoghurt before it has set.

Small-scale commercial production of yoghurt

Commercially produced yoghurt is, for safety reasons, invariably made from milk that has been pasteurized and cooled.

For a small-scale producer, it is important to make a consistent product. This means that a routine production system needs to be followed so that each batch has the same degree of set, flavour and appearance. To achieve this, the use of commercial starters is necessary together with temperature-controlling devices. Attention also has to be paid to presentation and packaging.

It is recommended that a source of commercial yoghurt starter is found. Laboratories of universities or ministries can often assist. It is normally supplied in small packets of freeze-dried culture which has to be allowed to grow in a small amount of milk for 8–12 hours before being added to the main bulk of the milk.

The steps in yoghurt-making are:

o pasteurize milk and then cool to 42–45°C;
o add about 1 per cent starter and mix in well;
o pour into plastic pots, cartons or jars;
o incubate until set (usually 3 to 6 hours) at 42–45°C;
o close pots;
o store in a refrigerator until sale.

Efficient low-cost incubators can be made from a wooden box lined with sheets of

Table 12. Temperature and incubation time for yoghurt

Temperature	Incubation time
40–45°C	3 to 6 hours
35–37°C	15 to 20 hours
Below 30°C	At least 24 hours

expanded polystyrene insulator. The temperature in such incubators can be kept constant between 42 and 45°C by suspending a light bulb inside; the exact wattage would have to be found by trial and error as it depends on the size of the box and local climate. Table 12 shows how important the incubation temperature is and how lower temperatures would reduce the volume made per day.

Commercial yoghurt is normally incubated in the pots in which it is sold. While traditional clay pots are still used, they are increasingly being replaced by small plastic ones sealed with either push-on caps or heat-sealed foil lids. Small heat sealers are available for this purpose and an example is shown in Figure 29. After sealing, the product should ideally be stored in a refrigerator to retard fermentation and prolong the shelf-life of the product.

Figure 28. An improvised incubator

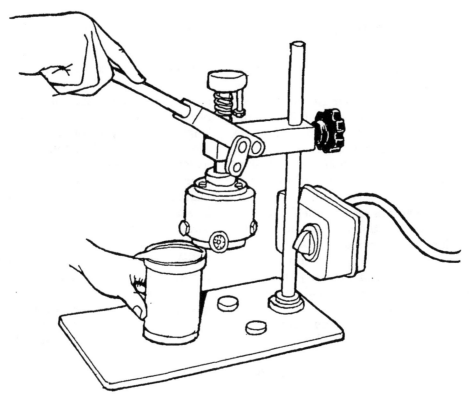

Figure 29. A simple yoghurt heat-sealing machine

4
Socio-economic considerations

MANY MILLIONS of people throughout the world own livestock from which they derive some or all of their livelihood. As a result, there is a wealth of indigenous knowledge about milk and milk products, and current practices, based on much innovation and adaptation, have evolved over many years. The role of women in this process has been vital. In many societies women are responsible for milking livestock and for the preparation and distribution of dairy products. Improvements in dairy production can build on this knowledge and diversity, and have the potential to increase options for the women involved.

Working with dairy producers to increase their technological choices involves three stages: understanding the context, identifying constraints, and planning options.

Understanding the context

An understanding of the conditions in which dairying takes place is important since cultural, social and economic contexts can vary greatly from place to place and can have considerable implications for any planned change in the production system.

First, the *cultural* context: milk and dairy products have cultural significance in different societies. In some communities, milk and milk products are a kind of social currency and are given as gifts which help to cement social relationships. In this way, milk can have an important non-economic role in society.

Taste is a significant factor in dairy production and one which is very culturally specific. It is not impossible to introduce new flavours and products to an area, but 'improving' the processing of a particular product – for example in terms of hygiene – may have a considerable impact on the flavour which could drastically reduce demand for that product. The cultural context in which milk is produced needs to be understood before improvements are planned.

Second, the *social* context: gender relationships within the household are an important part of the context in which dairy production takes place. Women are frequently involved in milking animals (and in some cases caring for them on a day-to-day basis) but may not always have control over any profit made from the sale of dairy products. Those who do control profits may not be able to buy or sell livestock as they wish.

Changes in the production system may alter gender responsibilities or gender relations: there are examples of a shift in control over a product which has become of greater economic significance in the household. For example, if dairy production and processing become a major income earner, rather than a supplementary income, control of the profit may shift from women to men. If women are responsible for providing food for the family (which is very often the case) this shift in control could result in poorer nutrition for the children.

Third, the *economic* context: milk is often produced primarily for home consumption, in some pastoral societies forming the mainstay of the diet, with the surplus sold for cash. Improvements in dairy production could divert milk from home consumption into a marketable product. This can have a serious impact on the nutritional health of the family, if the profit is not used to buy equally nutritious food. Malnutrition is common among pastoral communities moving from a milk products diet to an inadequate carbohydrate (e.g. maize) diet.

In addition, there may be economic (and other) benefits associated with current practices which are not easily identified at first. For example, Nigerian Fulani women derive benefits from selling their butter and cheese direct to their consumers, wealthier women in the nearby town, rather than to an intermediary: the women may receive gifts from their customer, as well as opportunities for joint business activities and access to land (Waters-Bayer, 1992). Waters-Bayer also describes how their current marketing strategies provide Fulani women with the opportunity to share news and information, and to relax together.

Recognition and understanding of all these contextual factors enables the development of appropriate options in partnership with women dairy producers.

Identifying constraints

All planned interventions ideally respond to a need expressed by the producers themselves and dairy processing is no exception. If, therefore, the women producers experience no problems in their current system, changes should not be planned automatically. On the other hand, if the women have identified constraints to their dairy production, discussions can then progress to where exactly the constraints lie. If the need is for increased income, it should be considered whether dairy production can meet this need, or in fact whether another income-generating activity might be more

suitable. It should be the women themselves who identify the constraints to dairy production, based on their knowledge and experience; outsiders should fit into their way of decision-making.

Constraints may occur at any one or more of the stages involved in dairy production and it is important to identify exactly where they occur, otherwise changes could be made which destroy the strengths of the current system.

First, there may be difficulties with *production*: for example, insufficient quantities of milk may be produced, due to the limitations of fodder, health or management; the seasonal nature of production may produce a bottleneck in processing; or lack of control or access to the livestock and their products may constrain production.

Second, constraints may be found in *processing* milk products: the techniques used may entail very hard work, or require equipment that is difficult to obtain; it may be difficult to process milk products at the rate required by market demand, or in the quantities required to make the enterprise profitable, because of the many constraints on women's time.

Third, *marketing* strategies may encounter difficulties, for example, irregular demand, interest or lack of interest in new products, maintaining or improving quality, requirements for certain flavours, requirements to meet certain hygiene standards, and so on.

When the women have clarified the problems which they encounter in dairy production, discussions can begin to identify options which may overcome them.

Planning options

At this stage it is important that the women clarify their objectives in the proposed activity. These will not necessarily be based solely on increasing profitability, but may also include labour or time saving, an increase in quality or ease of marketing, and so on. The role of extension agents should be to increase women's knowledge of the different options available to them, and to help identify the most appropriate activity to tackle constraints and achieve objectives agreed by them.

Bearing in mind the wealth of traditional knowledge on this subject, and the number of stages in production which could be focused on, improvements could be made to dairy production in very many different ways.

'Improvement' does not necessarily entail an increase in the scale of production or a shift to modernized levels of hygiene, but could instead involve a broadening of the product base, the introduction of other traditional dairy commodities, changes in the organization of production, or the introduction of new marketing networks.

The focus should be on increasing rather than restricting technological choices for women producers. It is important that women are able to learn for themselves about the different options which are available. Exchange visits and other mechanisms for sharing information on 'traditional' techniques and technologies within and between developing countries can play an important role in this process (Simaraks et al., 1991).

Whatever improvements are planned with the women, however, there are certain aspects which need to be considered (as with all development initiatives with women producers), as follows.

Time

One of the first considerations is women's time. An increase in the scale of production, or level of marketing, or more elaborate processing, will very frequently require a greater time input from the women producers. Women's time is always scarce, and has to be juggled between numerous domestic and productive tasks, and many women simply do not have extra time to invest in improvements, unless they are relatively wealthy and can afford to pay for help. This may also apply to short-term time investments, for example in learning new skills, taking part in training courses and so on. Women's time constraints may also vary with the season, which will affect their capacity to take on extra work at peak times of the year.

Linked to this question of time is the factor of women's family responsibilities. Many women have evolved ways of working (either as individuals or in groups) which enable them to combine a number of tasks – for example processing milk at home while looking after small children. A change in location or the amount of involvement could jeopardize this fine balance. However, some improvements in processing could save time and, provided the financial investment was not too high (see below), these might be of benefit even if they did not yield greatly increased profits. Other improvements may be more easily combined with current tasks, which would appeal to women. Ultimately the women themselves are the best judges of opportunities and constraints on their time.

Financial resources

The ability to invest in improved processes or technology will depend largely on a woman's financial resources. Many poorer women will not have the necessary income to do so, and must rely on credit. The availability of credit frequently depends on factors such as location (proximity to towns), levels of numeracy and literacy (rural women generally have lower educational levels than men). However, women who are working together in a group may find it easier to obtain credit than individuals. The projected profitability of the improved enterprise must also be taken into account. This can be determined by first calculating the existing profit: the total costs (including fixed costs – rent, loan repayments, and variable costs – materials, labour, transport) subtracted from the gross income, i.e. the total amount of money received for all the products sold (if no records are kept, this can be determined by estimating the level of production and multiplying by the price). The result is the net income. Potential profit can be determined by following the same calculation but replacing the gross income with the projected increase in sales, and by increasing the costs by the amount of the new investment. A comparison between current net income and projected income will allow for a decision to be made as to whether the potential profit will justify the increased time, money and effort required by the improvement, in economic terms. In this context, the question of end-use of the product is significant. If most of the dairy processing takes place for home consumption, the projected profit will be small if it exists at all; in contrast, a woman who processes largely for sale could potentially recoup her investment over time with increased sales.

Materials and equipment

The availability of the relevant materials and equipment should be considered in planning improvements to dairy processing activities. This should also include availability of repairs and replacement parts where relevant. In particular, improvements in hygiene should be planned with a good understanding of the women's access to the necessary resources, for example transport, or water and power supplies (as well as the implications for taste,

mentioned above). If these resources are not easily available, or supply is likely to be erratic, then alternative measures which are more reliable should be considered. In this case, alternative traditional methods of hygiene, well developed in other areas (see, for example, Unifem, 1993), may be appropriate, and some simple research or a number of exchange visits might confirm the possibilities for transferring these ideas.

Social roles and organization

The manner in which decisions are taken which affect the dairying process may provide opportunities or constraints to improvements in production. Sometimes the formation of a group (or indeed working with an existing group) may facilitate the organization of production; in other cases, this group action might eradicate benefits to the individual, some of which may not be immediately discernible (see above). The most appropriate form of organization, preferably building on current practices, should form the basis for improvements. The history of the many women's groups which have failed to generate income for their members is well documented and the automatic formation of groups which are not based on local cultural norms and organization should be avoided.

Ownership

The importance of understanding gender relations within the household with regard to access and control over livestock, their products and the profit from the sale of dairy commodities has been discussed above. If a household invests in new equipment, the woman may not retain control over it and this can affect both the running of the business and the enthusiasm and commitment of the women. Relationships between households, as well as within them, should also be considered, including extended family and neighbourhood ties which may impinge on any new investment or activity.

Skills and training

It is vitally important that any improvements in dairy processing build on women's considerable existing knowledge and skills. This will ensure a greater degree of self-reliance and sustainability. The requirements for training in new skills should also be identified. These may include not only technical training, but also perhaps literacy, numeracy and accounting skills. However, when planning any training, it is important to take into account the many demands on women's time. Women may not, for example, be able to go away to attend a full one-week course, and may prefer training to be spread over a number of weeks, close to home. Training courses held in the local language and the provision of child-care are both imperative if women are to take full advantage of possible improvements in their productive activities.

Marketing

Any planned improvements in dairy processing activities must be preceded by a study of current and potential markets. Existing marketing strategies should be studied to note their strengths and further potential (including the non-economic benefits outlined above). In particular, any proposed changes in the marketed product, or in the nature of the marketed product (for instance, a change in flavour resulting from different processing techniques) should be fully tested with current and potential customers before full production is established.

The potential for increased sales at a more distant or more centralized market must be set against the costs and reli-

ability of transport, as well as the social contacts mentioned above. In a number of countries, notably India, collective milk centres have been set up to facilitate milk marketing. These have effectively served to extract milk from the rural areas to service the urban centres and have failed to benefit most poor producers (Robinson, 1989). The producers can become dependent on a distant market over which they have no control, and must conform to standards of modern hygiene which hamper their profitability. The shift from individuals or small groups, marketing dairy produce locally, to centralized marketing systems should therefore not be made without very careful consideration of the factors outlined above.

Monitoring and evaluation

Any extension activity should be monitored by all the parties involved, as an integral part of the development cycle. Regular discussions and reflections with the women on whether the activity is meeting the objectives previously determined is vital if the activity is to continue to respond to women's needs. Such analysis can help to identify difficulties and allow adjustments to be planned.

The monitoring and evaluation of such activities should not focus solely on their implementation, but also include their impact on poorer and more marginalized individuals, as well as more general considerations such as gender relations, women's time burden, and so on.

The wealth of knowledge and experience of dairying provides great potential for work with women dairy producers, in ways that can increase their options and strengthen their control over their own production and processing, through learning from other dairy producers in particular, and finding ways to overcome the constraints which they face.

Checklist for increasing options for milk processing

The following checklist is intended as a guide for discussion with women dairy producers during the initial stages of planning. It is based on the points outlined above.

Understanding the context

Are women currently involved in dairy processing activities?	yes/no
Are the women unhappy with their current production system?	yes/no
Has the cultural role of milk been discussed?	yes/no
Has the social role of milk been discussed?	yes/no
Have the gender relations surrounding the control of milk products been discussed?	yes/no
Are milk products produced mainly for sale (as opposed to home consumption)?	yes/no

Identifying constraints

Are there constraints in the production system:

Is fodder a constraint?	yes/no
Is livestock health a constraint?	yes/no
Is livestock management a constraint?	yes/no
Is seasonality of milk production a constraint?	yes/no

Are there constraints in the processing of milk products:

Is time a constraint?	yes/no
Is the quantity produced a constraint?	yes/no
Is the technique/equipment a constraint?	yes/no

Are there constraints in the marketing of milk products:

Is quality a constraint?	yes/no
Is hygiene a constraint?	yes/no
Is lack of demand a constraint?	yes/no
Is transport a constraint?	yes/no

Planning options

Do women have the time to:

○ attend training courses?	yes/no
○ build/collect new equipment?	yes/no
○ spend on increased production/processing activities?	yes/no
Do women have the financial resources to invest in new activities?	yes/no
Do the women think that the projected profit of new activities (compared to current net income) would justify the required investment?	yes/no
Do the women have access to equipment, materials and supplies (e.g. transport, power) which might be required?	yes/no

Are the women organized in appropriate ways for developing their
 productive activities?   yes/no
Will the women have control over any income they may make, and over
 any new equipment?   yes/no
Will the women have access to the skills and training they will require?   yes/no
Is there a market for new/different products or increased levels of production?   yes/no

If the answer to the majority of the questions above is 'yes', then more detailed investigations and discussions with the women about improvements or alterations in dairy production may be appropriate.

5
Case studies

Buttermaking using an internal agitator, Ethiopia

TRADITIONAL ETHIOPIAN BUTTER is always made from soured milk. Small quantities of milk are collected in a clay pot over a period of a few days and allowed to sour naturally. When sufficient milk has been collected the milk is churned by shaking the pot until butter granules are formed. The churn is shaken to and fro either on the lap or on the ground.

This traditional method of churning is time-consuming and may take over two hours to complete. In making butter from sour whole milk, the objective is to extract the maximum amount of fat from the milk and convert it into butter. The buttermilk is then used for the production of a cottage-type cheese, called *ayib* in Ethiopia. As there is a big price difference between butter and cottage cheese, any butter fat remaining in the buttermilk must be considered an economic loss to the smallholder.

The efficiency of buttermaking by smallholders may be measured by the length of time it takes to churn the milk and the amount of fat extracted or recovered from the milk. Observations of smallholder traditional buttermaking indicated that efficiencies should be improved to save time and to improve the economic returns to the smallholder.

ILCA (International Livestock Centre for Africa) Dairy Technology personnel set about developing a device which, when fitted to the traditional clay pot, would give rapid and consistent agitation to the milk (shown in Figure 23, Chapter 3). This internal agitator has gone through several phases of development over the years.

Before recommending the internal agitator to the smallholders, it was necessary to carry out carefully controlled trials comparing the traditional with the new method. These involved churning sour whole milk with different levels of fat and different churning temperatures.

The results indicated that the efficiency of churning was considerably improved when using the internal agitator, which gave 76 per cent fat recovery against 67 per cent by the traditional method, and which reduced the churning time by more than half.

In separate on-farm trials, the internal agitator also performed very well against the traditional method.

One of the main factors affecting churning efficiency and, in particular, butter fat recovery is the temperature of the milk at churning. Using the improved design and a churning temperature of 18°C, fat recovery was 76 per cent, while at 25°C fat recovery was 55 per cent. These results highlight the advantages of using a low churning temperature and the internal agitator.

(O'Connor, 1992)

Village dairy development in the Occupied Territories, Jerusalem

Palestinian society has over the last 2000 years developed a village system of domestic food production with goat and sheep herds at its centre. From their milk are produced the traditional Palestinian dairy products of yoghurt, milk and white cheese which together with olives, lamb, vegetables and bread form the basic family diet.

After years of occupation, Palestinian efforts are now committed towards the indigenous rebuilding and development of their community. With the disruption of traditional gender roles, women have found themselves in the new role of providing for families which the men have left behind. Social and community involvement, once foreign to Palestinian women, has become an important lifeline as they assist one another in their survival. Committees were set up and projects were undertaken, one of which is a revival of the traditional cheesemaking which has been in decline.

The newly created Palestinian development institutions addressed the needs of women by organizing community-level training in the villages and supporting domestic dairy processing using goat and sheep milk and modernizing indigenous practices. Thus, the traditional white cheese was restored to its important place in the family diet with the women now trained in its production and preservation. Training was conducted on indigenous cheesemaking, while the practices and methods of generations before were revised and updated. Changes, such as filtration and pasteurization, were introduced but the age-old method of brine-salting has again become a common household practice, providing cheese for the family throughout the year.

With the success of household food processing, the women's movement moved on to the market place and social sphere, once solely the areas of men. At present, the women are exploring village-based development of processing facilities, col-

lective farming and dairy projects, and developing new integrated village farms, plans intended to create self-sufficiency for the Palestinians.

Using the latest research in animal husbandry and dairy practices, the new village-level programmes of integrated and complementary development are models for self-reliance and sufficiency by returning to the traditional ways of earlier generations, particularly in the area of dairy processing.

(Howard, Allan)

Goat-cheesemaking and marketing, Chile

The goat forms the basis of the subsistence economy of the poorest in the country. Goats provide milk, cheese, fresh and dried meat, as well as leather. These are used in the home and are also produced for sale. On a smaller scale, and depending on the availability of water, cereals and vegetables are grown.

There is a clear division of work between the sexes, with women being responsible for looking after the cattle, especially milking and cheesemaking. Men have traditionally been in charge of selling, and the women do this only when the men leave their communities in search of work.

Before the start of the project in 1990, dairy producers faced serious technical and marketing problems. Cheese production was hampered by lack of hygiene, plumbing, equipment, correct instruments, and technical knowledge about how to impove the process. On the marketing side, producers were dependent on an intermediary who went from house to house buying the cheese at the price that he decided upon. Prices fluctuated and were generally low.

With support from FAO's Latin American and Caribbean Dairy Training Regional Team, dairy factories were built in four communities, involving 194 families, with credit requested from INDAP (Ministry of Agriculture).

Each of the four communities has built its own cheesemaking factory, using traditional local materials. The walls are earth, mixed with some cement, and the roofs are asbestos or zinc. The walls, doors and roof have been painted with a plastic paint, except for the processing and maturing rooms where lime dissolved in water has been used, as it stops fungi. Wooden shelves were built and drinking water has been installed. Large quantities of water are used to cool the milk after pasteurization and to wash and clean the plant. Owing to the scarceness of water in the area, the water is re-used for irrigation.

These factories are enabling producers to make a better-quality product and, in time, they hope to be able to market their cheeses under more favourable marketing conditions.

In addition to the four plants, a Marketing Centre has been set up as a cooperative with the cheese plants as members. The centre has maturing and preserving units and packaging and reprocessing equipment. Its functions are to:

o receive cheese from the plants, check quality and maturity and, when necessary, allow the cheeses to mature;
o reprocess cheeses which are not up to standard;
o package the cheese for marketing;
o develop new products for the market.

The cheese is sent to town markets where it competes with other high-quality cheeses. An important achievement has been to obtain a Hygiene Certificate for each cheese plant.

When milk is brought into the cheese factory, it is first checked for quality and then filtered. The milk is pasteurized by heating to 63°C, kept at that temperature for 30 minutes and then cooled to 32°C. Coagulating agents (calcium chloride and lactic culture) are added to form the curd, and the whey drained off. The curd is then cut, shaken and heated, any remaining whey is poured off and ordinary salt is mixed in. The cheese is then moulded, pressed, dried and salted with concentrated brine and left for later sale, or to mature in the appropriate room.

Each of the cheese factories is equipped with the following:

o a 250-litre cheese vat (bain-marie) with an inner and outer wall, a stainless steel sieve and tap;
o an industrial cooker and two gas cylinders;
o a water heater;
o five 50-litre milk/whey jugs;
o two pairs of scales;
o quality control equipment;
o a plastic drum for the brine.

Each factory also has a dishwasher, worktable, curd cutter, press and moulds.

In each cheese factory, there is a cheesemaker and two assistants. Most of the workers are female and have been trained specially for the job. Producers have increased their incomes by between 50 per cent and 70 per cent as a result of taking the milk to the plant and being paid immediately. The maximum distance between the producer and the plant is no more than 20km.

The plant makes a profit based on the difference between the price paid to the producer and the sale price to the head office. Any profit, after costs, is distributed among the village community once a year. As part of the project, training and technical assistance are given to all members of the community. The number of women attending these courses has been increasing. The technicians encourage them to attend, since their participation is crucial to the aims of the project.

Those in charge of the project maintain that an important achievement has been to free the women from having to make the cheese, giving them more free time. However, the women themselves have not been asked whether they consider that their situation has really improved. They have apparently lost control over the making of cheese and the income from it. They need to be asked whether the higher price paid for unprocessed milk compensates for this.

(Soledad Lago, 1993)

Goat and milk production, Argentina

Most of the rural population of Argentina lives in the north-west, one of the country's poorest areas where about 62 per cent of homes lack even basic amenities. As a result, men are constantly migrating in search of work. The project is in Santiago del Estero in the Garza and Robles areas and is financed by the Foundation for Development, Justice and Peace (FUNDAPAZ), which has been working in this region since 1982 supporting communities or *campesino* groups. The goat project is supported by the Interamerican Development Bank and forms part of its special small producer development programmes.

The aim of the programme is to produce goat's milk in the irrigation area and then make goat's cheese which complies with health and hygiene regulations. To achieve this, the project is providing technical assistance and training in organizational skills.

To date, 26 rural producer groups have been formed, each one with a representative. They are affiliated to the Goat Breeders Association, which in turn is part of the Santiago del Estero Campesino Movement (MOCASE).

The main beneficiaries are the women who, from the beginning of the project, have played a central role in productive activities. They also act as representatives for their groups. Many of the men in Santiago del Estero are absent either temporarily or permanently, and women take full responsibility for looking after the goats and making cheese. Women are also involved in other FUNDAPAZ projects in the area and make shoes, clothes and sandals to be sold in the local markets.

The project has built a processing plant with a capacity to process 5000 litres of goat's milk a day. This produces between 800 and 1000 kilos of different types of cheese a day. The types of cheeses include semi-hard, grating, ricotta, cheese containing pepper, and feta which is preserved in brine. The cheese is marketed in cities such as Buenos Aires, Tucuman and Santiago del Estero, and has also been exported to Italy. One of the aims of the project is to hand over the cheese-processing plant to the Goat Breeders Association. Future plans include supplying the plant with a freezer for meat and a tannery for hides.

There have been great improvements in the equipment used. Pens for the female goats and kids, milking stools and milk cooling containers have been built. Each community has a veterinary medical kit containing internal and external anti-parasitic medicine, antibiotics, anti-diarrhoeics, medicine to treat the feet, etc. Special importance has been given to feeding and the diet is now supplemented with, for example, wheat bran and fodder in irrigation areas. The flocks have been improved by the introduction of better animals, pure anglo-nubian males and interbred animals at different levels of interbreeding. The project has also established alfalfa seed beds which has not been done in the area before.

An unforeseen result has been that organizations encouraged by the project have now been able to sell other products such as meat, eggs, vegetables and sausages at fairs in the city.

(Soledad Lago, 1993)

Rural women's milk production, Bolivia

The project, carried out between 1983 and 1991, involved eight communities from the Ingavi province in the department of La Paz, in the Tiahuanacu zone, 70km from the capital. UNIFEM financed the project and SEMTA (Women's Technical Services) was the executing organization. The region is 3000 metres above sea level; the climate is dry and cold and there are harsh frosts. Irrigated land is scarce and, on the whole, suitable only for annual crops. The inhabitants are of Aymari origin and still maintain their traditional customs.

The project aimed to improve cattle by artificial insemination, address aspects related to organization and technical training, and validate the role of women in the productive system to recognize their importance and participation.

Although men and women do an equal amount of agricultural work, the overall responsibility is taken by the men. The cattle belong to the couple while the woman takes care of them, helped by her husband and children. It is seen as part of her domestic chores even though it is often one of the main sources of income from selling milk, cheese or the cattle themselves. Both men and women are generally involved in selling although, when large sums are involved, the man usually assumes control.

Women have less access than men to education, and most cannot speak Span-

ish. This has in the past prevented them from speaking in public or actively participating in organizations. In general, they participate politically and economically only when their husbands are away or if they are widowed with young children.

The role of bilingual (Spanish-Aymara) women experts has been vital to the project. They come from peasant backgrounds and work full-time in the communities, analysing and explaining the technologies demonstrated by the technicians. The Milk Producer Communal Associations together founded the Tiahuanacu Producer Association. This latter was affiliated to the Milk Producers Association in La Paz (APLEPAZ) which works only with organized producers. From the beginning, the directors of the Communal Associations were mostly women, both locally and regionally, this being the only case within APLEPAZ.

Cattle stock was improved by a programme of artificial insemination, started in co-ordination with the Kallutaca Artificial Insemination Centre, part of the La Paz Development Corporation (CORDEPAZ). The plant provides semen for Holstein and Swiss Pardo cows at subsidized rates and also supervises the inseminators. Up to 1990, there was a 62.12 per cent success rate. Since 1986, continuous vaccination and parasite campaigns have been carried out, aimed also at sheep, goats, and pigs.

Some 210 family stables have been built as well as 25 large sheds to store and preserve the fodder. In addition, 14 Supply Centres, divided between the eight communities, were built to facilitate the marketing of milk. Roads have been widened and improved so that a milk collecting lorry could enter. All the work was carried out by the communities.

The milk marketing board (PIL) agrees to take the milk as long as certain requirements are met, for example, to ensure a daily supply of 1000 litres, to repair intercommunal roads and set up Supply Centres.

The producer groups insisted that PIL registered the women and not the men as the producers, as a way of recognizing the work done by the women to generate income for the family, as well as helping to facilitate access to credit and participation within APLEPAZ's organizational structure.

PIL donated scales and vats to safeguard the milk until the milk lorry arrived. Each centre has 'suppliers' who work shifts so that all the jobs are done. The women are in charge of the payroll, hygiene, requesting payment for milk, and making sure that charges and discounts are correct. All these different jobs, now done with ease, are the result of long training, including literacy training.

Throughout the project it has been clear that to guarantee recognition and empowerment of the women, it was not enough to focus only on production. As a result, the issue of gender has been present in all the project's activities. The literacy and training programmes have played a fundamental role in this. Training has been carried out through discussions, small courses, workshops and practical demonstrations, mainly in the Aymara language and at various levels.

The project has registered a 20 per cent increase in income from selling milk and cattle improvement compared with the amount previously received from selling cheese. An additional benefit is that producers receive money regularly every fortnight. One must also add the time saved for the women by not making cheese since, by selling to PIL, milk delivery can be done by the children or husband.

The women do continue to make cheese for their own households and still occasionally sell it, especially when the price of cheese rises, at times of low milk production, or simply when cash is needed.

It has been calculated that an average family delivers 125 litres of milk a month, which in 1991 assumes an income of 34 dollars, equivalent to the country's minimum wage. However, there are families who deliver up to 674 litres, which means an income of 182 dollars, i.e. five times the minimum wage. It has been noted that the greater the participation in the project, the greater the production of milk. An important achievement has been the quality of the milk, the fat content varying between 3.9 and 4.1 per cent. The average calculation by PIL is 3.5. The project's social impact is shown in the organizational structure created as a result of its intervention. This is made up of three levels: eight communal organizations formed by one or more Supply Centres, an Area Association comprising the Communal Associations, and affiliation to the Regional Association. Setting up these milk-producing organizations, mainly made up of women with the power to negotiate with PIL, has allowed for the identity of the women as producers to be recognized, by their own communities as well as by themselves.

(Soledad Lago, 1993)

Traditional sweetmeats, Bangladesh

The traditional production of sweetmeats called *mishti*, made from milk solids, is the biggest dairy processing industry in Bangladesh and in West Bengal. There are some 60,000 *mishti* production shops in West Bengal alone. In the rural areas of Bangladesh many small *mishti* producers are mainly from the Mindu Ghosh and Modak communities who are traditionally involved with milk and milk products, but most of these producers have no permanent shop. In towns, many tea stalls and restaurants sell *mishti* in addition to other products. As most *mishti* making is in the informal sector it is very difficult to estimate its turnover, but it provides jobs in all bazaars and is the biggest milk and sugar consuming sector.

The size of the *mishti* sector can perhaps be judged from the volume of milk imported, which has risen from Tk110 million (1977/78) to Tk4140 million (1989/90). This is despite the fact that liquid milk consumption is very low, about 14g per person daily. Use of huge quantities of milk in the *mishti*-making sector is blamed for creating this situation. The government is thus considering imposing some restrictions on making *mishti*. In the draft National Livestock Policy, for example, it has already been proposed to introduce a 'sweetmeat-less day' at least once a week in big towns.

There are dozens of types of *mishti* available in the market and most of the famous producers have their own speciality.

Mishti are an essential part of Bengali culture and heritage, and are used in some religious ceremonies and all private and official functions. It is a common gift to friends and relatives.

Some places in Bangladesh are famous for their particular type of *mishti* and, when someone visits these places, they are entertained with the speciality and usually take samples home.

Mishti seems to be becoming more and more popular as indicated by the several *mishti* chain stores flourishing in Dhaka and other big towns. These spend a considerable amount on advertising in the mass media. Bombay Sweet's competition advertisements, for example, were published regularly for several years in a widely circulated national news magazine weekly and are very popular among the readers.

A typical *mishti* recipe is:

Channa, acid-precipitated milk solids	1 kg
Sugar	300–500g
Cardamom	few pieces
Food colour, turmeric is common.	

The first step is to prepare the *channa*. The raw milk is strained and then boiled for 2 to 5 minutes over a fire. It is then briefly cooled and sour whey, saved from a previous batch, is then added. Care and skill is needed to add the correct amount of whey at the right temperature, generally 82°C. Too much whey produces a sour flavour, too little a pasty *channa*. The milk coagulates and the watery whey separates. The *channa* is then filtered through a fine cloth and hung up to drain.

As has been noted, there is serious concern in Bangladesh about the rising milk import bill and for this reason several development organizations are examining the possibility of using soy milk in *mishti* making, soya being widely promoted in the country. For more than a decade a local NGO, Gono Unnayan Prochesta (GUP), has been working to introduce soybeans in its working area. From its early days workers of the women and children programme of GUP were involved in the development and diffusion of recipes for domestic home use of soybeans. They were able to develop several recipes including soy-coconut *sandesh* (a candy-type sweetmeat) but their efforts to make a soy *mishti* were abortive, owing to colour, flavour, and textural problems. GUP's food-processing programme has been working on the development of good quality soy *mishti* in order to:

o develop sustainable food-processing enterprises for employment generation of poor men and women;

o reduce the country's dependency on imported milk powder;

o reduce the use of valuable liquid milk in making *mishti* and similar foods, so leaving it available for consumption by vulnerable groups;

o make available a low-cost alternative raw material for the *mishti* industry without reducing the quality of the product.

Experienced sweetmeat makers were involved and now a *mishti* using 70 per cent soy *channa* in dark coloured *mishtis* and 50 per cent soy *channa* in white *mishtis* has been developed. The quality of the product has been evaluated by experienced sweetmeat makers and they ranked it above commercially available *mishti* prepared from skimmed milk powder which is the adulterant most widely used in place of fresh milk *channa*. Market tests of soy *mishti* have been carried out and a group of women have been trained to make soy *channa* and soy *mishti* independently.

They are now in commercial production. The main problem identified was the *mishti* shop owners' reluctance to use soy *channa* because milk was cheap in the working area of GUP; in fact about 50 per cent cheaper than in the city market. Also the *mishti* business was very competitive, so nobody was willing to take the risk of selling soy *mishti*, fearing it would hamper their good will. All these production shops use defatted *channa* and skimmed milk powder as adulterants in making *mishti* without informing the consumer, so it is expected that they will also use soy *channa*, which is better than defatted *channa*, provided soy *mishti* becomes better known in the market.

Basic steps in making soy channa
o Soybeans are soaked for 8–12 hours. The weight doubles during this time.
o The soaked soybeans are blanched, in a perforated bucket or pan, for 1 to 3 minutes by dipping them in boiling water.

Blanching destroys enzymes that are responsible for the development of beany flavours. Longer blanching produces an inferior soy *channa* that is not suitable for production.

o The blanched beans are peeled by rubbing, washed and ground several times on a stone. Boiling water is added to facilitate grinding.
o The ground paste is added to a large pan containing boiling water and stirred thoroughly.
o The mixture is next filtered using a fine cotton cloth. The residue can be used for making different foods or can be dried and used as a poultry feed.
o The resulting soy milk is removed from the fire and a quantity of soured, fermented cow milk whey is added and mixed well. The milk coagulates immediately leaving a clear whey.

The coagulated mass is kept for about half an hour and is then strained using a fine cotton cloth.

The soy *channa* obtained after several hours of hanging is kept for 10–20 minutes under pressure to remove excess whey.

(Abu Ahmed Shamim, 1993)

Mala milk, Tanzania

Nronga Women's Co-operative Society Limited is located in Nronga village on the slopes of Kilimanjaro in Tanzania. In the local community, women rarely own land or other property. Dairy cattle, for example, are usually owned by men although, traditionally, women take care of livestock, milk the cows and market the milk. This milk is an important source of income for the family, under the full control of the women.

In 1985, 75 Nronga women decided to form a co-operative to market their fresh milk in Moshi, the nearest town. Four years later, 351 women had joined the co-operative and were delivering 500 to 1000 litres of milk per day. The enterprise was not, however, able to market the fresh evening milk which was also available. They approached TechnoServe to develop a method to process and store the milk to make marketing easier and more profitable.

Technoserve was able to use its experience with the production in Kenya of *mala* milk, a yoghurt-like fermented milk product consumed as a beverage or as part of a meal. The technology used is very simple and does not require sophisticated equipment. The fresh whole milk is filtered, sterilized by heating to 90°C and then cooled in a water bath. All this takes place in standard 50-litre aluminium milk cans. When the milk has reached room temperature, a *mala* milk culture is added to start the fermentation process. The fermentation process takes about 20 hours. The final product is poured into half-litre plastic bags and heat-sealed. Without refrigeration, the *mala* milk has a shelf-life of about ten days. It fetches 15 to 40 per cent more than the wholesale price for fresh milk. In the words of Ndugu Helen Usiri, chairwoman of the Nronga Rural Co-operative Society in Tanzania, 'cultured milk can stay longer while looking for a market'.

TechnoServe is still supporting the women of Nronga. Its project staff train co-operative members in *mala* milk production, quality control, accounting, marketing and general management. Recently, the co-operative members appointed a full-time manager who will be responsible for day-to-day management, accounting and administration of the enterprise.

Production and profits are still increasing. Nronga *mala* has found a receptive market, not only in Moshi but also in the more populous and distant cities of Arusha and Dar-es-Salaam. At present, all the spare milk is processed into *mala* milk and the women sell 250 litres of the new product a day.

The Nronga Women's Co-operative continues to be a highly visible and successful example of efforts to increase women's income and productivity. The project is often cited by the Tanzanian government and development agencies in the field as a model of sustainable development. As far as the women themselves are concerned, the *mala* milk co-operative increases their self-esteem and provides a source of income.

(Lazarraga, 1993)

Glossary of terms

Adulteration   The addition of other substances to milk, most commonly water, which reduces its quality

Casein   The principal protein in milk which is coagulated during cheesemaking

Churning   Agitating whole milk or cream to make butter

Coliform   Group of harmful gas-forming bacteria associated with unsanitary conditions

Curd   Coagulated milk solid

Enzymes   Naturally occurring substances in foods responsible for the development of rancidity, colour changes, separation, etc.

Fermentation   Process by which milk sugar is converted to lactic acid, causing the milk to sour

Incubation   Creating suitable conditions for the development of micro-organisms

Inoculation   Adding a culture of specific micro-organisms (a starter) to accelerate the fermentation process

Lactose   A type of sugar found in milk

Mastitis   Inflammation of the udder, usually in cattle

Pathogen   A micro-organism which causes disease

Pasteurization   Heating milk just enough to kill harmful micro-organisms without destroying flavour and nutritional qualities

Pastoralist   Sheep or cattle farmer

Polystyrene   A plastic with good insulating properties

Rancidity   Chemical reaction of milk fat causing rank and stale taste

Rennet   Substance found in the stomach of ruminants causing the milk to coagulate

Starter   Culture of micro-organisms added to milk to accelerate fermentation process

Sterilization   Destruction of all living micro-organisms

Whey   Watery part that remains after the milk has curdled

Equipment suppliers

The following companies can supply equipment for small-scale milk processing. The list is not intended to be exhaustive, and mention of a particular company does not infer that its products are recommended above other suppliers.

India

Dairy Udyog
C-229A-230A
Ghatkopar Industrial Estate
L.B.S. Marg.
Ghatkopar, Bombay 400086

K.S. Seetharamaiah & Sons PVT Ltd
29/1 Jaraganahali
10th K M Kanakapura Road
Bangalore 560078

Laksmi Milk Testing Machinery Co. Ltd
A90 Group Industrial Area
Wazirupa
New Delhi 110052

Mamko Project Engineering &
  Consultancy
Yashodham Office Complex
Gen. Arunnkumar Vaidya Marg,
Goregon, Bombay 400063

The Netherlands

Gebr. Rademaker
P.O. Box 81,
3640 AB Mijdrecht

United Kingdom

R.J. Fullwood & Bland Ltd
Ellesmere
Shropshire SY12 9DF

R. & G. Wheeler
Hoppins
Dunchideock
Exeter EX2 9UL

Armfield Technical Education Co. Ltd
Bridge House
West Street
Ringwood BH24 1DY

J.J. Blow Ltd
Oldfield Works
Chatsworth Road
Chesterfield S40 2DJ

Jankle & Kunkel Ltd
P.O. Box 16
Lewes BN7 3LR

Chadwicks of Bury Ltd
Villiers Street
Bury BL9 6B2

USA

Lehman Hardware & Appliances Inc.
P.O. Box 41
4779 Kidron Road
Kidron, Ohio 44636

Institutions

Africa

International Livestock Centre for Africa, PO Box 5689, Addis Ababa, Ethiopia.

Central and South America

Ministerio de Agricultura y Ganadería, Dirección Nacional de Ganadería, Av. Amazonas y Eloy Alfaro, Quito, Ecuador

Asia

Central Food Technological Research Institute, Cheluvamba Mansion, Mysore 570013, India
Division of Dairy Technology, National Dairy Research Institute, Karnal 132001, India
Srivijayavisakha District Co-operative Milk Producers' Union Ltd, Visakha, Co-operative Dairy, Visakhapatnam 530012, India

Europe

Dairy Training Centre – Friesland, P.O. Box 85, 9062 ZJ Oenkerk, The Netherlands
Food and Agriculture Organization, Via delle Terme di Caracalla, 00100 Rome, Italy

Groupe de Recherche et d'Echanges Technologiques (GRET), rue la Fayette 213, 75010 Paris, France
Intermediate Technology, Myson House, Railway Terrace, Rugby CV21 3HT, UK
Ma'an Development Centre, Shulfat, Jerusalem, Israel
Natural Resources Institute, Central Avenue, Chatham Maritime, Kent, UK
Overseas Development Institute, Regent College, Regent Park, London, UK
Scottish Agricultural College, Food Science and Technology Department, Auchincruive, Ayr, UK
Small-Scale Dairy Technology Group, Rhodosdreef 154, 3562 TK Utrecht, The Netherlands
Swiss Centre for Development Co-operation in Technology Mgt. (SKAT), CH – 9000 St. Gallen, Switzerland
Swiss Federal Institute of Technology, Department of Food Science, Eisgasse 8, 8004 Zurich, Switzerland
University of Reading, Department of Food Science and Technology, Reading, Berkshire, UK

USA

United Nations Development Fund for Women, 304 East 45th Street, 6th Floor, New York, NY 10017, USA

References and further reading

Ash, Rita (1983) *Cheesecraft*, Tabb House, Cornwall, UK

Bachmann, M.R. (1984) *Fermented Milk in Dairy Development in Third World Countries*, FIL–IDF Bulletin No. 179

Bekele, E. and Kassaye, T. (1987) 'Traditional Borana milk processing', *ILCA Newsletter*, Vol. 6, No. 4

Biss, Kathy (1988) *Practical Cheesemaking*, Crowood Press, Wiltshire, UK

Black, M. (1977) *Home-made Butter, Cheese and Yoghurt*, A & C Black, UK

Carr, Sandy (1992) *The Mitchell Beazley Pocket Cheese Book*, Reed International Books, London, UK

Chavangi, N.A. and Hanssen, A. (1983) 'Women in livestock production with particular reference to dairying', FAO Paper on Expert Consultation on Women in Food Production, 7–14 December 1983, Rome, Italy

Demeruen and Renaud, J. (1971) 'Production and processing of milk under nomadic and transhumance system', paper presented at the Regional Seminar on Dairy Education and Dairy Development in the Near East, 4–5 October 1971, Beirut, Lebanon

Dingemanns, Bert (1992) 'Reducing contamination risks', *AT Source*, Vol. 20, No. 3, Agromisa Publication, The Netherlands

Dubach, Josef (1992) *A Lifetime of Cheesemaking in Developing Countries*, SKAT, Switzerland

Dubach, Josef (1989) *Traditional Cheesemaking*, IT Publications, London, UK

Dubach, Josef (1988) *Diez Anos del Proyecto Queserias Rurales del Ecuador*, FEPP, Quito, Ecuador

Ebing, Pauline and Rutgers, Karin (1991) Agrodok 36 'The preparation of dairy products', Agromisa, Wageningen, The Netherlands

Eck, A. (1986) *Cheesemaking – Science and Technology*, Lavoisier Publishing Inc., New York, USA

FAO (1990) 'The technology of traditional milk products in developing countries', *Animal Products and Health Paper 85*, FAO, Rome, Italy

FAO (1988) 'Village milk processing', *Animal Products and Health Paper 69*, FAO, Rome, Italy

Frazier, W.C. and Westhoff, D.C. (1978) *Food Microbiology*, 3rd edn, McGraw-Hill Books Co., USA

Jones, Rachel (1992) 'Cheeses made by direct acidification', *Indian Dairyman*, Vol. 44, No. 3, India

Karki, Tika (1986) 'Some Nepalese fermented foods and beverages', *Traditional Foods: Some Products and Technologies*, Central Food Technology Research Institute, Mysore, India, pp. 93–94

Kordylas, J. Maude (1990) *Processing and Preservation of Tropical and Sub-tropical Foods*, MacMillan Education Ltd, Hong Kong

Kosikowski, F.V. (1982) *Cheese and Fermented Milk Foods*, F.V. Kosikowski and Associates, New York, USA

Lazarraga, R. (1993) *TechnoServe*, Vol. 17, No. 1

Ministerio de Agricultura-INIPA (1986) 'Programa Nacional de Queserias – Informe de Evaluacion', Lima, Peru

Ministerio de Agricultura Y Ganaderia (1985) 'Proyecto Queserias Rurales del Ecuador', Quito, Ecuador

Ministry of Agriculture, Fisheries and Food (1987) 'Leaflet 437 – Farmhouse Buttermaking', MAFF Publications, Northumberland, UK

Ministry of Agriculture, Fisheries and Food (1983) 'Leaflet 849 – Quality Control of Farmhouse Dairy Products', MAFF Publications, Northumberland, UK

Mol, J.J. (1992) 'The world of milk processing', *AT Source*, Vol. 20, No. 3, Agromisa Publication, The Netherlands

Nalugwa, L. (1988) 'Keeping milk on the move', *African Farming*, September/October 1988

National Dairy Council (undated) 'Facts About Soft Cheese', NDC Leaflet, London, UK

National Dairy Council (undated) 'Facts About Yoghurt', NDC Leaflet, London, UK

National Dairy Council (undated) 'Making Cream on a Small Scale', NDC Leaflet, London, UK

Nielsen, E. and Ullum, J. (1989) *Dairy Technology I*, Danish Turnkey Dairies Ltd, Denmark

O'Connor, Charles (1992) 'Traditional cheesemaking in West Africa' *Food Laboratory News*, Vol. 8, No. 3, Germany

O'Connor, C.B. (1992) 'Improving the efficiency of buttermaking using an internal agitator fitted to a traditional clay pot', Dairy Technology Unit, ILCA, Debre Zeit

O'Mahoney, F. and Bekele, E. (1985) 'Small-scale manufacture of cheese from cow's milk', *Appropriate Technology*, Vol. 12, No. 3, IT Publications, London, UK·

Rangapa, K.S. and Achaya, K.T. (1975) *Indian Dairy Products*, Asia Publishing House, India, pp. 119–154

Robinson, Clive (1989) *Hungry Farmers: World Food Needs and Europe's Response*, Christian Aid, UK

Siegenthaler, Ernest (1968) *Two Procedures for Cheesemaking in Tropics and Emerging Countries*, University of Michigan, Michigan, USA

Simaraks, Suchint, Terdsak Khammaeng and Suthipong Uriyapongson (1991) 'Farmer-to-farmer workshops on smallholder dairy cow raising in three villages in Northeast Thailand' in: *Joining farmers' experiments: experiences in participatory technology development*, Haverkort, B., Johan van der Kamp and Ann Waters-Bayer, eds, ITDG, UK

Smeets, R. and Hameleers, A. (1991) *Economic Analysis of a Dairy Plant*, Small-scale Dairy Training Group, Utrecht, The Netherlands

Tamime, A.Y. (1985) *Yoghurt: Science and Technology*, Pergamon Press, Oxford, UK

Thear, Katie (1983) *Home Dairying*, B.T. Batsford Ltd, London, UK

Unifem (1993) *Women's Roles in Technical Innovation*, IT Publications, London

Van den Berg (1988) *Dairy Technology in the Tropics and Sub-tropics*, PUDOC, Wageningen, The Netherlands

Verma, I.S. and Mathur, B.N. (1986) 'Status of the milk products manufacturing technology', *Traditional Foods: Some Products and Technologies*, CFTRI, Mysore, India, pp. 58–70

Waters-Bayer, Ann (1988) 'Dairying by settled Fulani agropastoralists in Central Nigeria', *Farming Systems and Resource Economics in the Tropics*, Vol. 4, Wissenschaftsverlag Varik Kiel KG FR, Germany

Waters-Bayer, Ann (1992) 'Studying pastoral women's knowledge in milk processing and marketing – for whose empowerment?', paper prepared for the IIED/IDS Workshop 'Beyond Farmer First: rural people's knowledge, agricultural research and extension practice', 27–29 October 1992, IDS, University of Sussex, UK

Webb, B., Johnson, A. and Alford, J., eds (1974) *Fundamentals of Dairy Chemistry*, 2nd edn, Avi Pubs. Inc, USA

Whittier, E. and Webb, B. (1950) *By-Products from Milk*, Reinhold Pubs. Corp., USA, pp. 230–239

Zimmermann, S. (1982) *The Cheesemakers of Kafr Al Bahr: The Role of Egyptian Women in Animal Husbandry and Dairy Production*, Women and Development Series, Cairo, Egypt

www.ingramcontent.com/pod-product-compliance
Lightning Source LLC
Jackson TN
JSHW052134131224
75386JS00037B/1268